THE STRATEGY
IMPLEMENTATION GAP

James Bawtree & Michael Young

pmlogic®

James Bawtree

PMLogic

202b/39 East Esplanade, Manly NSW 2095, Australia

1800 763 881 / 0419 533 678

james.bawtree@pmlogic.com.au

CONTENTS

Introduction

OPENING THOUGHTS FROM JAMES

This book aims to help busy executives deliver their strategic goals in a sustainable, efficient and effective way through projects. It includes input from many of our readers and supporters — so thank you for overseeing and delivering projects and programs we have reviewed and optimised, attending our training courses, and interacting with us at conferences and workshops. All these touch points assisted us with the knowledge and the stories we have included for your reading pleasure!

So, to start with a story. In early 2018, an executive acquaintance mentioned to me informally at a networking event that he was moving to Brisbane, and had an interview lined up for a managerial role with a financial services company. He said that when thinking about his approach to the interview, he wondered "what would James do?" I replied: "A review." He said "yes" and added that a consultancy had recently completed a review of the company, which would be a great baseline from which to work.

When starting anything new, it is critical to measure the current environment before making any changes. It allows you to validate the measurable difference of any changes you do make.

We have seen many strategic plans beautifully crafted by a team of clearly very smart business executives, supported by equally smart consultants. The plans looked great and read well, but did not bear any resemblance to what was actually happening in the business executives' organisation.

Early in my career, as a very driven project engineer and then later as a project and program management consultant and trainer wishing to climb the corporate ladder, I observed this behaviour and thought it odd there was always a disconnect. The strategic plan's stated goals never seemed to align with the organisation's practices or achievements and this became my purpose — to professionalise project management from strategy to delivery. I hope you enjoy the book, and feel free to let me know your key takes-out or planned actions.

OPENING THOUGHTS FROM MICHAEL

Having worked with hundreds of organisations as a management consultant for more than 20 years, I have been constantly amazed, and also somewhat shocked, that almost all of them had major issues achieving their stated strategic goals or objectives. These organisations were all shapes and sizes and operated in many different sectors. They employed smart people and had executive teams that were great leaders, but something seemed to be missing.

The thought that just wouldn't escape my mind was: "Why can't these organisations deliver what they said they would?" This set me down a path of learning and reading about strategy, and its execution. I read almost every book ever written on the topic, as well as all the academic literature. I even started a PhD in the hope of finding an answer to this seemingly simple question. The more I read the more I came to realise there was a significant gap between an organisation defining its strategy, and then implementing it. The academic literature even highlighted this gap, and offered up different theoretical and conceptual models. However, many of those models were either impractical and therefore not overly suitable in the modern organisation, or they were incomplete, and only covered a very small situation, part of the organisation, or industry.

WHY WE WROTE THIS BOOK

The title, *The Strategy Implementation Gap*, refers to this misalignment, and the gap it causes between intent and actual achievement.

There are two key areas that cause this misalignment:

1. changes in the external environment
2. the inability of the organisation's people and other resources to deliver the objectives.

With an average 70% of projects failing to meet all their goals, large organisations are often behind their strategic plan at the end of the first year. This makes achieving the second year's objectives harder, and those for years three to five almost impossible. Because the strategic plan is set in stone, objectives cannot be updated. And often the CEO falls on their sword.

We have worked in project management-related roles and both of us have made a career out of using projects and programs to turn executives' plans and ideas into a practical reality. We wrote this book to show the implementation of strategy, using much of the learning from the art and science of delivery. This book is a culmination of more than 40 years of practical experience, combined with extensive research of the literature written on this topic.

Chapter 1
WHY IS THERE A STRATEGY IMPLEMENTATION GAP?

Today's executives can no longer stay on top of their game while trying to run businesses that achieve an incremental revenue increase each year. Organisations and their staff can't survive on incremental returns. A corporate longevity study[1] found that in 1965, the average tenure of companies on the S&P 500 was 33 years; by 1990, it was 20 years, and it is forecast to shrink to 14 years by 2026. On top of this, about 50% of the S&P 500 will be replaced over the next 10 years by companies that we probably have not heard of yet.

"Business as usual" (BAU) is no longer a sustainable approach. Customers have increasing demands for new features and functions, competition has never been as intense, and pressure to reduce costs or increase margins through the use of offshore or gig-based workers is disrupting traditional business models.

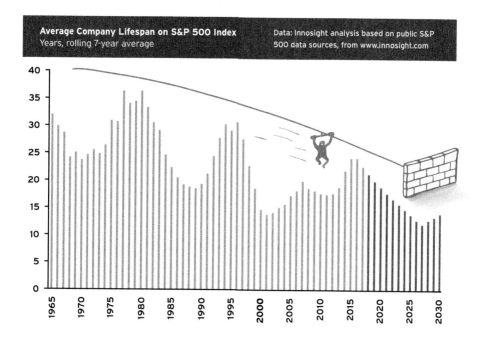

Average Company Lifespan on S&P 500 Index
Years, rolling 7-year average

Data: Innosight analysis based on public S&P 500 data sources, from www.innosight.com

To stay relevant, executives need to transform their businesses, sometimes cannibalising very profitable products with newer ones, such as Apple did by replacing the iPod with the iPhone before sales started to decline. After all, Apple's slogan was "Think Different". A modern way of analysing this approach would be to say the iPod was an MVP (minimum viable product) that helped continue the funding of the iPhone until it was ready for launch in 2008.

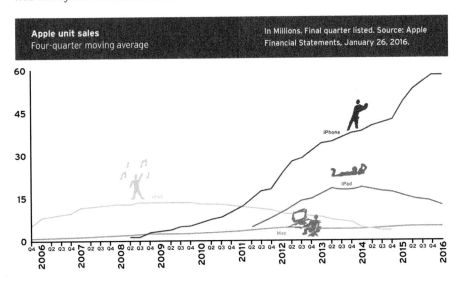

One of the key problems for executives is the structure of organisations. The current typical hierarchical structure of divisions, branches or units and teams, reduces the agility of organisations to respond to market forces, as well as ideas. On top of this, we see most organisations have a separation between BAU or operations teams, and project teams, further fragmenting decision making and the possible speed of change.

We often observe executives trying to manage a huge workload covering operational matters as well as project activities, and often failing to do both. It is revealed in delayed decision making, or time spent firefighting.

Are you one of these executives? A good way to check is to print out your diary for the week and note in red all the ad hoc meetings and issues that you manage, then on Friday look back and assess the percentage of planned meetings, as opposed to unplanned meetings.

Did you have a greater level of unplanned meetings? If this is the case, then I would put it to you that you are an ineffective executive. The reason: if you are asked to attend a meeting, with little or no preparation, and required to make decisions on the spot, then the likelihood is that most of those decisions will be ill-considered and with hindsight, wrong.

Think about times you have had to decide on the spot without sufficient information. Do you agree? Do you also agree that this impacts your ability to meet your goals and the broader organisational goals?

¹http://www.innosight.com/innovation-resources/strategy-innovation/upload/Corporate-Longevity-2016-Final.pdf

Chapter II

ORGANISING WORK IN THE AGE OF DISRUPTION

Sociologist Tom Burns and research partner psychologist George Macpherson Stalker coined the phrase "structure follows strategy". As part of their studies they suggested one of the key requirements for successful implementation is putting in place an organisational structure supporting the strategy. But it is not just the organisational structure you need to look at, it is far more fundamental than that. As an executive, you need to examine the way in which you organise people's work, how each person in the organisation operates, and the structure of teams, departments and branches.

To understand the structure of today's large organisations, let's take a short tour through the history of organisations and make a brief stop at the Industrial Revolution.

Much of the pre-industrialised world revolved around farming and small cottage industries. The blacksmith operated a small shop to make and repair tools and horseshoes. Weaving and textile production was common. The butcher, the baker and the candlestick maker operated small businesses employing a few people from the local village. Farmers grazed livestock and grew crops, fruits and vegetables that were sold at the local markets. Wheat was taken to the local mill and ground to create flour, and bakers bought it to make bread. At the time, simple machinery was powered by people, or animals that pulled ploughs through the field or were hitched up to drawbars in the mill to turn the large grinding stones.

With the introduction of steam and mechanisation — industrialisation — factories were set up to produce large quantities of fabric. Hundreds of largely women and children were employed to operate this machinery. Productivity soared and outputs increased 100-fold. Factory-based manufacturing and production soon spread to other sectors and with improvements in steel, electrification and the use of coal to fuel industrial machinery, mass production accelerated.

From this time, academics, and philosophers started examining these factories, seeking not only to understand them, but to optimise production and develop the best structure and organisation for the industrial firm. Through studying the nature of the work itself and applying scientific techniques to management, researchers were able to maximise productivity and output, and make organisations more profitable.

A key aspect of this scientific approach was the organisation of people, or labour, and the nature of the work each person performed. The "father of modern economics" Adam Smith in his *Wealth of Nations* (1776) identified that specialisation and concentration of workers on their single subtasks often led to greater skill and greater productivity than would be achieved by the same number of workers each carrying out the original broad task. The "sage of Kirkcaldy", Scottish social philosopher and leading figure of the Enlightenment advocated for the establishment of hierarchical structures with sections of people at the lowest level performing a unique set of specialist tasks. Soon after, German philosopher Immanuel Kant suggested that all crafts, trades and arts profited from the division of labour. Kant believed that when each worker stuck to one kind of work that needed to be handled differently from all the others, they could do it better and more easily than when one person did everything. Where work is not thus differentiated, and divided, where everyone is a jack-of-all-trades, the crafts remain at an utterly primitive level.

More than 100 years later, German sociologist Max Weber suggested bureaucratisation was the most efficient and rational way of organising human activity. His ideal bureaucracy was characterised by:

- hierarchical organisation
- formal lines of authority (chain of command)
- a fixed area of activity
- rigid division of labour

- regular and continuous implementation of assigned tasks
- all decisions and powers specified and restricted by regulations
- officials with expert training in their fields
- career advancement dependent on technical qualifications
- qualifications evaluated by organisational rules, not individuals.

Industry soon entered the era of hierarchical structures and bureaucracies. In bureaucratic organisations, communication and information flows in hierarchies, up and down the chain of command, not horizontal between key people across the firm. To gain agreement with managers in other departments, often the bosses of these different divisions needed to be involved in discussions with their peers in the other department. This took time and involved many people in many conversations, but it is important to recognise that during this hierarchical development the business environment was very stable and the future was clear and easily predicted. Technology change was limited and competition between similar organisations was even more limited.

Today's modern organisation is structured much like the factories of yesteryear. But rather than labourers and factory workers operating machinery, instead we have knowledge workers using computers, email and corporate systems.

Many of the expectations and reward and incentive arrangements we use today stem directly from the Industrial Revolution. Individuals start in low-paid positions and seek promotions to more senior positions. Junior technical people are promoted to senior roles, senior technical people are promoted into management roles and managers are promoted into executive roles. In the past, an individual used to work for the same business for most of their life and over time was promoted to more senior roles.

The notion of a career has dramatically changed. Today there is a lot more movement between organisations, with individuals taking on more senior roles with each move. Nevertheless, careers still exist for many people and the expectation of promotions and pay rises has not gone away.

The benefits of a bureaucratic structure break down when the operating environment is turbulent, rapidly changing or variable in nature. Organisations that don't adapt rapidly enough are subject to disruption (see Chapter VIII). Bureaucracies also don't respond well to innovation or the need for new activities or products. The structure itself has been established to perform and refine a discrete process or operational activity for which the people undertaking such work have developed methods and personal systems.

PROJECTS

Recognising the challenges of strict hierarchies, organisations over the past few years have moved towards matrix structures with cross-functional teams delivering new products and new services, changes to the way of working, and the implementation of new business systems. Projects are the vehicles used, and are a way of organising work and people who have a single focus on delivering a specific outcome or result for the organisation. A skilled project manager is appointed to lead the project team comprising individuals with specific skills drawn together from across the organisation.

Projects are temporary structures established and resourced for a specific purpose and then shut down once this has been delivered. As temporary organisations, the project team members can be assigned specific roles and put into boxes on an organisation chart. Their purpose can be clearly articulated within a business case, so that projects are able to be understood and valued by their permanent counterparts as helping them adapt and adjust to the changing environment. At the end of the project, staff assigned to it are either sent back to their department, or in the case of temporary staff and contractors, they leave the organisation.

The modern organisation has an internal structural dichotomy. The organisation is ambidextrous, containing projects that are vehicles of change, and operational hierarchies are used for stability and efficient delivery of processes. Both projects, and operations, are necessary to the success of the organisation, as each provides specific benefits and delivers specific results. Projects deliver change, new products, or services that did not previously exist. Operations deliver well-known and refined processes as efficiently as possible.

Given the nature of projects, and given they are delivering previously unknown changes, products and services, they require a different management approach than that used in operations. Projects focus on schedules, resource management and delivering specific outcomes or benefits to the organisation.

Project-based work also requires a different mindset. Individuals require an action bias, and work to deadlines to deliver agreed outcomes. That is not to say operations don't have deadlines or don't deliver outcomes, these two metrics are the raison d'etre for project teams. Those in the project management field will talk about the triple constraint — time, cost and quality. These constraints are often referred to as the iron triangle, as projects often have all three variables fixed in an attempt to deliver a known outcome in a precise time frame and budget. This can leave little flexibility to absorb changes needed to maximise the project's outcome. It is important to unlock one or more of these constraints, so the project team can maximise the desired outcomes and optimise the project schedule and budget, rather than focus on the technical elements of the projects, such as inclusion of a specific function.

As Charles Darwin famously wrote in his *Origin of Species*: "It is not the most intellectual or the strongest of species that survives; but the species that survives is the one that is able to adapt to and adjust best to the changing environment in which it finds itself." Your organisation needs to adapt to its changing environment and the best way for organisations to control these changes is to use projects.

As a high-performing modern executive you should use projects to transform your business.

We do three types of jobs here ... *Good, Fast and Cheap.* You may choose two!

If it is <u>Good</u> and <u>Cheap</u>, it will not be <u>Fast</u>.

If it is <u>Good</u> and <u>Fast</u>, it will not be <u>Cheap</u>.

If it is <u>Fast</u> and <u>Cheap</u>, it will not be <u>Good</u>.

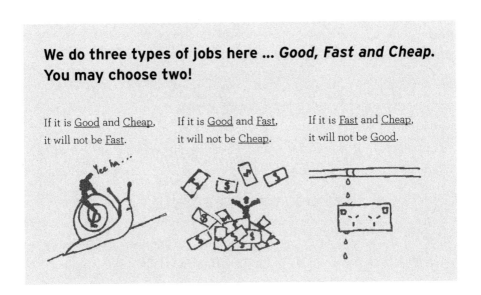

Chapter III
ALIGNING STRATEGY IN A RAPIDLY CHANGING WORLD

To fully understand the challenges of strategy implementation in a rapidly changing environment, we first need to examine the concept of strategy.

WHAT IS STRATEGY?

Derived from the Greek word *strategos*, strategy is an ancient concept often expounded through the ages in a military context, and refers to a plan of action designed to achieve a particular goal. Modern corporate strategy was created out of military and naval structures and theories. Ancient Chinese general, military strategist, writer, and philosopher Sun Tzu, the British East India Company, and 19th-century Prussian general and military theorist Carl von Clausewitz were often referenced. Their strategies have been applied to the business domain since the British East India Company, but especially as companies formed as a result of the Industrial Revolution.

The application, however, especially from the mid-20th century has not been consistent because there are different interpretations of strategy. It has become an all-purpose term applied to a range of management techniques, theories, concepts and corporate issues that are subject to fads and fashion. It is a term used to describe lofty, important or wide-ranging concepts and is also considered analogous to terms such as guiding motives, matching of the internal and external environments, or a series of actions. Wright, Kroll and Parnell provide the most appropriate definition of strategy: "... top management's plans to attain outcomes consistent with the organisation's missions and goals."

Strategy can operate at the corporate, business unit and functional levels of an organisation. Corporate strategy is concerned with enterprise-wide decisions in diversified organisations and relates to the industry sector and markets in which it competes. Corporate strategy deals with growth (through acquisitions, new ventures or organically) and divestments, diversification or retrenchment. Corporate strategy is often represented as the portfolio of businesses for investment and formalised as a document to co-ordinate effort at the business-unit level. Business-unit strategy focuses on a firm's method of competing within an industry or market and is concerned with achieving a competitive advantage over rivals. At the functional level, strategies focus on short and medium-term plans within each department, ensuring they contribute to the overall corporate objectives. These include strategies for marketing, new product development, human resources, finance, legal, supply chain or IT.

There is no recognised "one best way" of developing strategies or strategising, however the most dominant approach is described by Canadian academic and author on business and management, Henry Mintzberg, as the "planning school" of strategy. These are explained in detail in Chapter IX. Planning is forward looking and requires clear articulation of intentions, supported by formal controls, to ensure plans are consistently pursued in an ever-changing environment. Typically, strategic plans are developed for the medium to long term, covering a period of three to five years. The process of strategic planning starts with a formulation by the planning staff, approved by top management. The plans are then decomposed so lower-level tasks can be scheduled and allocated to specialised areas of the organisation. The strategy is then implemented by operational staff, often in complete isolation from those who formulated or approved the strategy. The planning school, however, began to lose favour in the 1980s. The regimented strategic planning process failed to develop any true strategic choices and produced virtually no results.

The Jack Welch story is instructive. He started at US conglomerate General Electric as a junior chemical engineer and rose to be CEO and chairman, and was famously known during the early 1980s as "Neutron Jack" for eliminating employees while leaving buildings intact. Welch popularised so-called "rank and yank" policies used now by other corporate entities. Each year, Welch would fire the bottom 10% of his managers, regardless of absolute performance. He rewarded those in the top 20% with bonuses and stock options. Welch believed the planning system had evolved from being fresh, ideas-oriented and effective, to becoming bureaucratic and inhibiting. To increase "candour" and constructive discussions, planning reviews were restructured. Welch and the two vice-chairmen talked with individual strategic business unit members privately and informally. Rather than focusing on comprehensive strategic documentation or planning concepts, Welch directed the review around the key issues for each business. Welch eventually cut the 200-person corporate planning staff in half. His objective was to get "general managers talking to general managers about strategy, rather than planners talking to planners".

The key reason for the demise of the planning school approach generally was the misguided assumption that a formal plan could provide long-term guidance. Planners did not entertain the possibility that the environment could not be predicted with any great accuracy and that the plan would be of no use because it could neither be implemented nor be useful even if it were implemented. It became widely accepted that formal plans either decayed, or required constant adjustment during periods of turbulent environmental change. Some changes occurred so rapidly that the organisation focused all its efforts on constantly re-planning, with strategy implementation never actually occurring.

With rapid change in the environment, as we discuss in Chapter VIII, the planning process had to be simplified, and well-thought-out strategic plans became nothing more than an extrapolation of existing patterns, or were copied from standard industry recipes.

A seminal 1994 publication explains why research into strategy implementation has not made much progress. The article, "The rise and fall of strategic planning", described the failure of strategic planning to produce the expected results despite decades of intensive effort. Mintzberg, and fellow academic James Waters, suggested disruptive change had rendered ineffective the analysis of past trends as a technique to predict and plan for the future. As a result, firms steered away from deliberate and planned approaches, and relied instead on adapting strategy over time to reflect changes in the business environment.

Does this mean using a top-tier consultant to develop a strategy by running a series of planning workshops at a nice resort is dead? Perhaps. These workshops might be interesting, but quite often they descend into a "chat fest" and the resultant plans are often rapidly developed by an executive team with little buy-in from their organisation and with little or no experience of delivery. A better way is needed.

THE ADAPTIVE STRATEGY

A shift to a more agile and adaptive approach to strategy creates some real challenges for executives and their organisations. The old-school approach of developing a great-looking plan that contains lofty goals and a vision for the future, are long gone. Many firms look to create a strategic plan that proposes multiple horizons over which key changes and initiatives will be implemented, but due to the changing environment, the initiatives themselves can be a priority one minute and then seemingly no longer relevant the next.

Leading organisations develop a bi-modal strategic plan that contains both fixed and variable elements. If the strategy is set over a five-year period, then the longer-term goals to be achieved over the whole period should be static, and the medium and short-term actions are adjustable. This allows the selection of key initiatives to evolve based on organisational learnings and to adjust to the changing environment, and helps confirm that the organisation is on track to deliver against the long-term objectives. This way, long-term assumptions about the future are not needed, and a more certain, less volatile and clear plan can be put in place and adjusted each quarter or even once or twice per year.

Some large organisations go part of the way, falling into the trap of resetting their objectives each year and not checking what has been delivered in the plan. Although this allows more realistic plans each year, it does not allow the organisation to learn and adjust. Implementation can also become an afterthought, so while the objectives get adjusted, delivering the actual initiatives becomes largely a "wish", and very little is delivered.

To deliver an adaptable strategy, a more flexible and agile structure is required. Projects provide the perfect vehicle to do this. In Chapter XI we will discuss more about how this is achieved by using Program Logic.

THE STRATEGY IMPLEMENTATION GAP

Aspiring senior executives go to top universities and business schools to learn how to develop winning strategies that will deliver a sustainable competitive advantage. Yet, despite the most senior people in the organisations conjuring up the most elegant of strategies, defining a suite of goals to which to aspire, and identifying a scorecard of intelligent key performance indicators to track their progress, many companies don't ever deliver on their strategies.

"82% of Fortune 500 CEOs feel their organization did an effective job of strategic planning. However, only 14% of those same CEOs indicated that their organization did an effective job of implementing the strategy."
Forbes Magazine

A key barrier to successful implementation is a poor or vague strategy. The strategy itself must be actionable and implementable. Often the strategy is poorly written, containing either a wish-list of outcomes the executive wants to achieve, or maybe a series of "motherhood statements" that are not specific. When the strategy is poorly articulated, vague or does not contain implementable outcomes or initiatives, it is impossible to execute, even by the best team in the world with an unlimited supply of time or money. Often the lack of clarity results in middle managers not understanding what the strategy is and what senior management wants done. This can result in confusion, as well as differing interpretations of what the strategy is, which creates uncertainty as to how to best deliver it.

"A poor plan executed now is better than a perfect plan executed next week."
George S. Patton

Implementation is a disciplined process that takes a logical set of connected activities and turns the organisation's strategy into reality. Without careful planning and the right level of resourcing, strategic goals will not be achieved. We have found that often when reviewing people's day-to-day activities in different business units, it is apparent there is a significant disconnect between the strategy's suggested priority, and the activities being carried out on the ground. Often, the strategy is written in such a way as to make it impossible to connect these activities to the objectives captured within the strategic plan.

This is referred to as the strategy implementation gap, and it is alive and well in most organisations.

Chapter IV
DIFFICULTIES OF STRATEGY IMPLEMENTATION DELIVERY

Often it takes substantially more time, effort and resources to execute a strategy than it does to formulate it in the first place. Implementation can be a difficult journey full of potholes, bumps and the occasional roadblock. Implementation also requires a good strategy to start with, and everyone across the organisation must understand the strategy and what they personally need to do to achieve it. Often the culture, structure and existing incentives create inertia and a resistance to change. This pushes back against the executive's desires to change. Development and formation of the strategy is the domain of the board and the senior executives, but often the implementation of the strategy is viewed as a tactical activity, and devolves to middle management to implement. This separation between the strategy and its implementation creates a disconnect between the executive and middle management, and sets up a potential conflict between those who develop the strategy and those who execute it.

Implementation is often an organisation's journey into the unknown to do something it often cannot clearly articulate. In a way, this situation may not be a surprise, as a lot more is known about strategy formulation than implementation. Much more is known about the planning than the doing.

Research by Lawrence G. Hrebiniak, Emeritus Professor in the Department of Management at The Wharton School of the University of Pennsylvania and a member of the Strategy Group shows there are a number of critical obstacles to successful strategy implementation. Hrebiniak has been on the Wharton faculty since 1976 and teaches courses in competitive strategy and strategy implementation in the MBA and Executive Education programs. Over the years he has received several awards for teaching excellence, most recently in 2008 for his MBA course, "Competitive Strategy". We can examine in turn the critical obstacles to successful strategy implementation.

INABILITY TO MANAGE CHANGE

An underlying human condition is a natural resistance to change. Doing something differently to the way it has been done for some time pushes people outside their comfort zone. It requires them to work against existing habits, preferences and mental models they have built up, sometimes over many years. This has the tendency to cause stress, requires a rethinking of the fundamentals of the job itself and often means the new way of working or new process can take a substantially longer period of time. Work builds up, which further exacerbates stress levels.

OVERCOMING INTERNAL RESISTANCE TO CHANGE

Change and transformation is a higher risk, as it involves a journey into the unknown. In effect, we are asking people in an organisation to forget what they have been doing for years and to operate in a different way using new processes they have not seen before or of which they have no experience. There is no guarantee the new way of working will be more efficient or effective or achieve the desired outcome. If no compelling reason for change is communicated and clearly understood by everyone in the organisation, resistance remains high and often each person quickly reverts to the old way of doing things.

But the challenge of internal resistance is not just confined to the workers, it also exists in the minds of middle managers and executives. Many managers and executives are concerned or even fearful of change, as any change from the regular routine has a potential for failure. Concerned managers and executives may resist these changes, driven by the subconscious fear that they may be blamed for the failure.

Managing change means not only keeping people happy, but also reducing resistance to new ideas and methods as well as knowing the tactics required to manage the implementation process over time.

SEPARATION BETWEEN PLANNING AND DELIVERY

Planning and implementation are often separated. This occurs because the development of the strategy is often carried out by the board or by the C-suite, and then once developed, the plan is passed to the management of the business to implement. This approach occurs as executives make broad and mistaken assumptions about how well the strategy they have in mind converts into understandable work at all levels in the organisation.

Hrebiniak takes a more cynical view. Based on his research of C-level executives, he identified they have an unspoken belief that it is their job to develop the plans and then the job of the presumably less smart managers to make the plans happen.

Planning affects implementation, just as the implementation of the strategy affects planning. As such, a simultaneous view of planning and doing is required. Implementation should not be an afterthought. Successful strategic outcomes are best achieved when those responsible for implementation area also part of the planning or formulation process.

From the CEO down, all managers need to roll up their sleeves and pitch in to make a difference. The content and focus of the roles of executive and middle manager will differ, however the focus and commitment required does not change.

IMPLEMENTATION TAKES LONGER THAN FORMULATION

One of top management's biggest blind spots is the failure to recognise that any significant shift in strategy requires changes in day-to-day activities throughout the organisation. These shifts can only be successful if implemented systematically, which can take a substantial amount of time.

The planning may take weeks, or possibly a few months, and often the implementation can take more than a year. Executives become impatient and want quick wins and expect immediate results that demonstrate action is being taken and progress is being made. This is partly because in their minds the strategic concepts seem to have been spoken about forever, and also due to the board's expectation of achieving immediate results.

Implementation is a process that takes time, and often involves a series of integrated decisions and actions. This requires more detailed tactical planning and involves substantially more people than does formulation. Goals and objectives need to be broken down into projects, programs or initiatives, which need to be planned in detail. Budgets have to be allocated and resources assigned. Each member of the implementation team needs to have a clear understanding of what is to be done, how it will be done, and have time allocated to deliver these projects.

The longer time frame also means executives can often lose interest, or their attention is diverted to the latest problem or the next big decision that needs to be made. It can also make it harder for managers to focus on and control the implementation process, as many things, most of them unforeseen, can materialise and challenge the manager's attention.

EXECUTING A STRATEGY THAT CONFLICTS WITH THE POWER STRUCTURE

Organisations are collections of people who work together. Individuals have desires for promotion, expectations of advancement and want to differentiate themselves from their peers. Our egos and inner thoughts drive our personal priorities and behaviours, which can at times be in conflict with the strategic goals of the organisation or counter to the strategies being pursued.

The maxim says "what you reward determines the behaviours you get". Individuals need to be incentivised and measured on achievement of strategy implementation. When this does not occur, there is no status afforded to, or personal desire created by, taking risks and potentially failing, which can be associated with delivering strategic programs.

POOR COMMUNICATION BETWEEN INDIVIDUALS AND BUSINESS UNITS

C-level execs are focused on their part of the organisation and delivering their own top priorities. The role of an executive is becoming more challenging with an ongoing requirement to do more with less resources, and achieve results in a less and less predictable world. It is therefore critical that executives build and empower their team, allow a level of (calculated) failure and learn from these failings so similar activities are not repeated in the future.

With an overwhelming level of communications through a variety of different channels from email, chat, and instant messaging, to SMS and voice, it is critical that many of the messages are repeated and sent through these multiple channels. It is also important that messages are communicated with the reader in mind, so they are quickly able to understand them in context, and the "call to action". The communicator's instructions must also be crystal clear.

LACK OF ACCOUNTABILITY FOR IMPLEMENTATION DECISIONS AND ACTIONS

The big "A" for accountability is always a challenge for organisations. It is much less risky for executives to not take on accountability. It means they can't be blamed when some activities fail to achieve their planned results. This lack of accountability has consequences such as decisions being pushed up to the top levels of organisations. This causes executives to spend most of their time in meetings, not having enough time to fully understand the issues being presented for their attention and therefore making uninformed decisions on topics they typically know less about than members of their team. This issue is further compounded by their lack of time to follow up to see if they are able to add any further insight because they are into the next meeting, making the next uninformed decision.

We also see a lot of committees in organisations and from our research it is really clear they are generally not effective decision makers. This challenge causes delays and impacts on key internal and external stakeholders to the organisation.

STRATEGY OWNERSHIP IS LACKING

When we help organisations improve their delivery model we ask staff what is their level of knowledge or ownership of the strategy? They will often cite the strategic plan but when questioned further are not familiar with the content, including high-level goals, and even less able to state how their activities help achieve these goals.

Linking strategic objectives with the day-to-day tasks and concerns of people at different organisational levels and locations is typically not done well. Many staff have no idea how their task will help achieve the strategic goals of their organisation, and the majority unfortunately do not care as they have become detached from their organisation's purpose. This often results in them not operating at a high-performing level and merely "attending" work to ensure a pay cheque.

When transforming an organisation it is important to reach as many stakeholders as possible. However, the larger the number of people involved the greater the challenge of effective strategy implementation. To combat these challenges, organisations must ensure a clear line of sight to strategic goals, and a joining up of activities and outcomes at all levels. This allows staff and stakeholders to understand how their tasks align, and therefore why they are important.

IMPLEMENTATION SKILLS LACKING

Competency to perform one's role is becoming more critical. This is due to the increasing pace of change and organisations needing to empower staff to perform in their roles. Where staff are not competent, as we often see with "accidental project managers", this has a significant negative impact on the organisation's ability to achieve its goals. Competencies should be defined by skills, measured by certifications, and experience measured by industry qualifications.

NO GUIDELINES OR MODELS TO ASSIST STRATEGY IMPLEMENTATION

Much of the literature on strategy implementation has examined and identified specific factors and models that either:

- lead to successful strategy implementation
- limit or create barriers to successful strategy implementation
- are required to be in place as precursors in order for a successful strategy implementation to occur.

Strategy implementation models proposed in the literature do not easily translate into models industries can use, or in practice, and therefore do not provide sufficient guidance for practitioners.

OPERATIONS VERSUS CHANGE

Organisational capability when it comes to change and transformation requires careful thought, because people have different skills. The teams need to be resilient, adaptable to change, have a high degree of autonomy and be comfortable with ambiguity. Often, we are brought into organisations where the program and project teams are struggling to keep up with the changes being requested of them, and their stress levels are sky high. This type of environment has a risk to the health of those in it, and without the right level of support often results in people getting sick and taking leave to recover.

The second issue is that organisations have largely been structured to deliver changes in alignment with a strategic plan that is static and set over a three-to-five-year horizon. The challenge is that most of these plans rapidly become misaligned to what the organisation needs to achieve, and is working on, so when there are key decisions to be made at the delivery level there is no valid reference to use to ensure these decisions are made using the right context. This causes confusion and long meetings to gain agreement on what is trying to be achieved.

MANAGERS ARE TRAINED TO PLAN, NOT EXECUTE

Managers learn about predictable operations and systems. Implementation is often not taught as part of MBA programs and in business schools, where the focus instead is on developing strategies. Many executives lack the skills and capability to successfully execute, implement or deliver their organisation's strategy.

Managers are trained to analyse the environment in which the organisation operates, identify key capabilities and develop plans for the short to medium term. Many executives have climbed the ranks or moved between organisations working mostly in technical, operational or sales roles. In these roles, people often deliver repeatable patterns of work and are not exposed to planning and executing longer-term initiatives.

Knowledge of implementation often comes from, as Elbert Hubbard stated, the "school of hard knocks" and the pathways to successful results are likely fraught with mistakes and frustrations.

Implementation is often regarded as a matter of operational detail, and thus may be perceived as beyond the purview of an executive. If managers are trained to plan and not to execute, then the successful implementation of strategy becomes less likely and more problematic.

Organisations are hierarchical and structured in silos; they are not flexible or agile enough. Implementation is "a mere detail of the planning process".

WHAT IS THE RESULT OF POOR IMPLEMENTATION?

There are many outcomes of poor strategy implementation. The immediate result is not achieving the desired goals or outcomes, but poor implementation also leads to other problems.

- Employees don't understand the way in which their jobs contribute to important implementation outcomes.
- Time and money is wasted because of inefficiency or bureaucracy in the implementation process.
- Implementation decisions take too long.
- The organisation reacts slowly or inappropriately to competitive pressures.
- CEOs are often fired due to poor implementation.

Chapter V

STRATEGY IMPLEMENTATION DELIVERY FRAMEWORK

We have worked with hundreds of organisations over many years and in that time have identified five key principles that underpin successful strategy implementation.

The five principles are: purpose, people, practices, platform and performance. These principles are required throughout each iteration or business cycle.

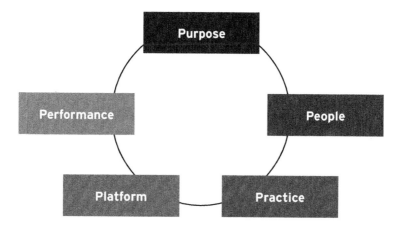

We will examine each of these in turn.

PURPOSE

What is the purpose of a business? It's a basic question, but it's not always easy to answer. While most businesses have their mission and vision statements detailed in their strategic plan and on their website, often this does not capture the true purpose of the organisation.

On first glance, many people consider the only aim of a business is to generate returns for shareholders, however this is a rather short-sighted and narrow perspective. Many of the financial services organisations failed their customers by taking this view, and enticing their executives with short-term incentives (STI) where they receive bonuses for achieving financial targets in a brief time-frame.

If is often said, people are a company's biggest asset. In a globalised marketplace, the war for skilled workers is tough, particularly with ongoing record-low unemployment rates. Harvard Business School research has shown that the millennial generation has a very different perspective when it comes to employment. The research found the millennials have a stronger social conscience and are willing to take up to a 30% pay cut to work for a firm that is socially and environmentally responsible.

Social media and advances in mobile phone technology have also brought a new era of transparency. A population armed with mobile phone cameras can capture any potentially unacceptable actions by individuals or organisations and broadcast them in an instant to millions. This has created a new form of activism that has gained traction through ubiquitous connectivity.

Customers, employees and shareholders no longer see exploiting the environment or specific groups of people for the benefit of company profits. A new age is dawning where stakeholders will publicly call out poor behaviour, vote with their feet and change brands to a competitor. Perhaps this is what you are contemplating?

The purpose of your organisation needs to be reflected in the strategic plan. The purpose needs to encapsulate your organisation's key value proposition. Why do your customers buy from or work with you? What is unique about your offering from their perspective? This purpose must also consider your employee and partner needs. It is also important to understand and communicate the greater goal your organisation aims to achieve that is beyond the product or service you provide.

Purpose should be the "north star" that can be used to provide direction for employees and partners and should communicate what your organisation stands for. Without a clearly articulated purpose, often an organisation spends a lot of its time solving the wrong problems, or even if it is working on solutions to the "right" problems, often in doing so it is causing harm.

This holistic or system of systems[2] based thinking is what we believe will really help your organisation set the right strategic objectives and create a compelling reason that appeals to the hearts and heads of your team and your clients.

Through the work we have done around the world we have found that many organisations have lost sight of their purpose. It is not clear why they exist beyond making money.

As a high-performing executive in this age of disruption, leading your team through a great pace of change, you must be mindful of the impact of these changes on other people in your organisation, supporting your organisation, or buying from your organisation. It is important not to blindly go through the motions, or ignore bad practices and behaviours.

Harvard Business Review[3] has reported that those employees with a giving mindset and desire to help others, the "extra milers", drive team performance. The same article also stated that 3% to 5% of an organisation's employees account for 20% to 35% of value-added collaborations. You must therefore make informed decisions on the tasks and activities that align to your social purpose as well as organisational goals.

In our consulting and training engagements, we come across clients who are just going through the motions. They do not appear to have purpose apart from achieving financial gain and domination of a market. They are organisations lacking that emotional element that holds the team through a belief in what they are doing, rather than just being technically capable. This culture often restricts organisational team members from feeling empowered, which can have dramatic psychological effects such as depression and a feeling that they are stuck in a rut and powerless to do anything.

One example is a technology company whose vision was to be the biggest in its region. When asked for its vision or mission, it was logical, but without emotion. The executives of this organisation would benefit from watching some of Simon Sinek's *Start With Why*[4], which we believe is one of the best sources of information about purpose. One of his books *Find Your Why*[5] guides you through the process of "why" discovery.

Purpose is your organisation's raison d'être. Please reflect on what you have just read or watched in the case of the Starts With Why video and think about your organisation.

Does your organisation have its purpose clearly stated?

PEOPLE

When we think of people we must think of organisational culture. Our organisations are made up of tribes sharing a common interest or purpose and as a leader it is your job to inspire your team into action, but it must be the right action. It is also important to empower your team to make decisions aligned to your vision, as opposed to constraining them to a specific approach and set of outputs with which they are not familiar, or with which they often don't agree.

A Gallup[6] study shows only 15% of employees are engaged in the work they do, and one of the two reasons is their manager. Carefully selecting the right person as a manager is critical. Only 10% are naturally wired to be great managers, and this can be assessed using an inherent personality test such as the Caliper Profile[7].

The other reason employees are not engaged relates to training, which should focus on education rather than measuring performance.

And then there are the millennials, In 2018 they represented the largest share of organisational labour force[8]. Only 16% see themselves with their current employer in 10 years. Their main reason for moving is lack of support/training in leadership, and being overlooked for leadership roles. The majority, 87%, also believe success of a business should be measured in more than financial performance, and 73% believe business should have a positive impact on society.

So what are you doing to address these needs?

We recommend providing a clear purpose for your team, and defining clear roles and responsibilities in a position or job description. Regularly discussing with them how they feel they are performing, and checking alignment with you and your organisational goals, are important. We also recommend you define career pathways for them and learning opportunities, which are critical to creating and maintaining high-performing teams. This sounds like a lot of work for each person. But much of this work can be automated within HR and workforce management platforms. We elaborate on this in the Platform section, later on in this chapter.

For organisations to be successful it is critical that employees' values align to their organisation's purpose, otherwise there is a complete disconnect. A cross-purposes in values can significantly impact people's psychology, causing at its extreme, depression, and at best, frustration, confusion and wasted work.

To reduce these challenges we recommend effort is put into clarifying your teams' roles and their alignment to your organisation's purpose. A simple solution is to organise into "tribes" of like-minded roles, for example, customer-facing, back-officing, your executive and your board or minister/s if in government agencies. Once you have grouped your teams into tribes it is important to ensure you have the right balance of internal versus external-focused tribes, as well as leaders, managers and doers. This capacity assessment will reduce blockages within your organisational system. One tribe completing their work quicker will cause a bottleneck and associated cross-team delays and frustrations, if your system is not optimised for throughput as a whole. It is also important to assess the organisational hierarchy from board or minister to "doer" level for similar bottlenecks.

In relation to hierarchy, your organisation should be regarded as a place of learning. It is critical that a coaching and mentoring process is in place. Organisational "elders" can coach and mentor those with less experience. Australia's indigenous peoples, at 50,000 years-plus Earth's longest continuously surviving civilisation, are probably the best example of this. Their people go through an initiation ceremony similar to university where they spend many months becoming an elder, or "learning grandma's secrets" as an Aboriginal fella told me when visiting Uluru recently.

We have also learnt that all people have natural abilities, which when leveraged allows them to perform at a higher and more sustained level than those people who have learnt the ability. Where you have inherited a new team, or are looking to recruit new team members, we have found that using a behavioural assessment tool such as the Caliper Profile instrument[9], helps ensure your team can play to their strengths and are supported in areas in which they are less naturally strong. Please note, this natural strength does not mean they can't achieve something in an area that is their weakness. That's just a matter of motivation. But it does mean that because they have to work at it, should their motivation disappear, then they are less likely to perform in the area.

It is difficult for organisations to always place people in roles in which they are strong. We have found transparency is a good motivating factor to keep them performing. This transparency can be achieved through having a strategy implementation platform that provides your team with information on their progress towards the goals and what they have committed to achieving. As we operate in a more and more complex environment we are recommending your organisation simplifies its technology architecture to reduce the number of interfaces and therefore complexity in architecture. This helps establish a key principle of a single source of truth for information from which reporting is done. It also helps your large stakeholder group understand the alignment of activities to outcomes and associated benefits.

PRACTICES

Practices are your approach to "getting stuff done". They are the processes you follow, and the skills and experience required of you and your team. Having environmentally sustainable practices and a good work/life balance for your employees will improve their performance and therefore your company's bottom line.

Your organisation needs to adapt more quickly to a rapidly changing external environment and workforce. In the gig economy, more and more of what your organisation does will be automated and the number of workers you employ will reduce as they are replaced by automation and temporary workforce. For these reasons, knowledge of your organisation's strategic objectives delivery practices is critical to being a high-performing executive.

At each of these three strategy implementation levels, portfolio, program and project, you must understand where you need to be actively involved in setting the vision, and making priority decisions where your teams can't resolve delivery constraints. You must also look to the future and help your teams at each level remove barriers to progress.

The changes your organisation needs to make to achieve its strategic goals are risky by nature, as they involve doing new things, working in new ways and working with new team members and customers, so having practices that are not over-bureaucratic, but also allow sufficient control, is critical.

Once you have ascertained your teams' roles and the principles to which they need to align, the next step is to assess their capabilities — their skills, experiences and competencies — to ensure these learnt or adaptable behaviours are optimised to produce the best results for your organisation.

The most thorough approach is to implement task management, that is, assigning tasks that need to be completed to your team members. If your team are undertaking routine and/or predictable tasks this can be achieved through assigning scheduled tasks to individuals. Where these tasks are less predictable, a list of tasks can be assigned to a team rather than individuals and they can help assess how long each task will take. Assigning tasks is only one aspect of successful practice management and we think of this as part of operational or project management. From an operational perspective, the tasks should be more predictable and therefore skills and effort required should be known. Where these operational practices are changing or being changed, then project management practices can ensure they are managed in an effective way to cause the least negative impact to achieving your organisational goals.

A program management approach helps you not only manage your many projects in an efficient and co-ordinated way, but also your on-going or operational tasks to ensure changes to them are optimised for timing and positive holistic contribution to your organisational goals. A good example of poor, or non-existent program management, occurs when, for example, the CFO mandates all staff use an IT system that has been optimised for accountants. Although the accountants are satisfied with the changes, the impact on the organisation is huge and negatively impacts performance. Another example is HR outsourcing performance management, learning and development, to already over-stretched and undereducated line managers. Again, this makes HR's work easier, but has detrimental impacts on organisational performance.

To link business or operational planning and your strategic initiatives, we recommend your organisation runs all activities as programs, with two types, those that are ongoing, and those that are changing the way your organisation operates. The planning of ongoing tasks should be done on an annual basis. In parallel, projects and programs that change business operations should be planned and delivered in a formal staged approach.

Organisations require a specific unit to develop and maintain the required strategy implementation "system". This is most commonly done through establishing a project management office. The SIO is a practice that helps your organisation co-ordinate programs and projects to ensure they align to strategic goals and deliver the value and benefits the organisation is seeking through its investment in such initiatives. A recent Australian Institute of Project Management (AIPM) study in conjunction with KPMG found organisations with a PMO are more likely to deliver their strategic objectives. From the work we have done in assembling and optimising PMOs, we know, when set up correctly, they reduce extra work and duplication across your organisational silos as a result of one silo completing its "project". But they don't take into account the way in which the new piece of the jigsaw fits within the overall organisational puzzle. An additional project therefore needs to be run to adopt the changes and ensure they fit. PMO management should also help stop projects and tasks that do not align to your organisational goals. It is a better management of resources, finances, and risks, and reduces the burden of corporate reporting. It should improve the management of information across the program or portfolio, if at a division or organisational level.

A current gap we are witnessing in organisations is the traditional approach to strategic planning, which focuses on goals for the organisation but not on how and/or if these goals are to be achieved or achievable. Here we strongly recommend your strategic planning includes program and project delivery expertise. We provide more information on these practices further on.

One surefire way of focusing on the right opportunities and problems is to, as Stephen Covey recommends, begin with the end in mind. Covey was an American educator, author, businessman, and keynote speaker, famous for his *The 7 Habits of Highly Effective People*. When helping organisations improve their performance, we leverage the Managing Successful Programmes[10] (MSP®) framework as one of the tools. The practices defined within this framework specify the need for a shared vision as well as a "blueprint", which is a description of the processes, organisation, tools and technology and information flows your target business model will have once the transformational program finishes, as well as at each major stepping stone within its lifecycle. Having this description of the target state/s helps identify current gaps and therefore ensures that work is done on the right things to achieve stated goals.

We also leverage the Lean Six Sigma framework; Lean helps minimise the touchpoints and Six Sigma helps ensure sufficient quality is achieved. The Six Sigma DMAIC is also useful to help define the problem and ensure the right measures are in place to support any change initiative. Blending this approach with the MSP® framework provides a strong foundation to commence changes and prove that effort is being expended in the right areas. It also helps define where the greatest opportunities or value can be had, and assists with prioritising what you do first.

PLATFORM

With the onset of the gig economy and more and more of your team represented by temporary and/or on short-term engagements, having a software platform that helps them find information in the right contextual location, following a workflow to be able to deliver their tasks efficiently, and selecting the right team members with the right competencies, cannot be left to ad-hoc manual process and therefore chance.

Most organisations have a plethora of software applications and uncontrolled spreadsheets and Lotus Notes databases that are being used for core business. This is especially true in the finance business units and their love of spreadsheets.

We would be interested to hear from you if you feel your organisation is different.

These applications are doing similar things but in different ways. This produces different hierarchies and formats from which data is difficult to extract and transform to allow other applications to load and make sense of.

Rather than focus on technology, it is therefore important to have an enterprise view of information — what needs to be stored and what needs to be reported. IT is information technology, but most organisations think about technology first and do a poor job of managing information.

By focusing on information first, your team are also able to better design a solution to secure sensitive information, such as personal data and company information, that a competitor could use to its advantage.

Taking a platform-based approach is more holistic then application by application, and linking to the objectives and goals you are looking to achieve will provide a significant competitive edge in this rapidly changing age.

Platform is all about automation — automation that will help your organisation deliver more, ensure quality outputs are achieved, reduce organisational risk and significantly assist with corporate reporting. Many tools have been developed to support strategy implementation practices stemming from IT and construction industries, and there are many mechanisms and systems for enterprise resource planning, traditionally in manufacturing industries, but now widespread. Strategy teams have corporate reporting tools such as Balance Score Card. Finance and HR teams also have a selection of tools to assist their focuses.

A missing toolset or system is the strategy implementation, which needs to take into account all of the above and integrate these tools and systems, rather than remain silo-based. We foresee strategy implementation tools as an emerging area. But we recommend you ensure they are an integrating tool, which allows you and your team to extract relevant data from other tools and systems. You can then transform it into contextual data aligned to your strategic objectives and the progress of your teams' projects to achieve your goals and load into it a corporate reporting dashboard to allow you and your executives to interact with the information.

A key decision with any tool or IT system is cloud and/or on-premises. We strongly recommend including cloud in your future enterprise architectural design, if it is not already. The cost savings are large, the performance better due to your vendors being able to maintain their applications for you, and you reduce your capital expenditure. You are also able to increase or decrease the amount of data storage space and licences you hold as your organisation adapts to better achieve its goals.

This approach allows your organisation to increase its performance by adapting your IT systems to your current needs rather than having to make decisions on hardware and software, which may be incorrect due to the rapid changes your organisation is experiencing.

One of these changes we have seen is in the field of collaboration. These changes have initially been driven by social media platforms such as Facebook and now there are many collaboration platforms available for organisations to improve the approach to sharing information and breaking down "stove-pipes". Information can be shared with your defined tribes or groups, which breaks down organisational divisional barriers, and can also extend to your third-party suppliers. Information stored in repository can be viewed through different libraries or catalogues tailored to your needs and information feeds (RSS).

The platform can track activities and we have learnt it is also important to track action in a central place. The level of workload on team members is transparent and can be balanced across teams. This transparency also allows your team to complete what they have committed to, such as actions from meetings. From our experience these are often deferred, typically due to good reasons, but we recommend setting realistic time frames for their achievement and being able to easily view what you have agreed to do, and perhaps having a friendly PMO staff member provide you a reminder where needed.

PERFORMANCE

Performance can only be assessed if you measure — and measurement requires agreed metrics. We recommend you ensure there are three levels of metrics being tracked in your organisation:

1. organisational
2. team
3. individual.

At an organisational level, these metrics need to focus on how the activities being performed by your organisation in the form of operational or ongoing tasks, as well as the change activities in the form of projects, align to achieving your strategic goals. We recommend that setting and monitoring these metrics or key performance indicators is done on a regular basis such as quarterly, so they can be adjusted to emerging needs and requirements as changes occur within the external environment.

At team level, these are the metrics that your tribes, divisions, groups and business units need to set and against which to assess their performance. We expect you have divisional and business-unit metrics and recommend these be broken down so all sub-areas such as business units, combine to make a division. When you add all the business unit elements, they should make up the whole of the divisional performance targets — no less, no more.

These targets can then be further aggregated up from division to group to make up the totality of the group's performance targets. An example of this we have seen effectively used is the Balance Score Card. For tribes that are cross-divisional teams, we generally do not see metrics on their performance and here we recommend you focus on the more humanistic metrics such as capability and capacity, career pathways and cross-team assistance.

At individual level, these are the personal performance metrics that must link into your organisational and team metrics. This is where a few well-chosen lead-based metrics are critical. One individual metric should align to multiple team and organisational metrics. This process takes time and you will certainly not get them all correct, so allow for flexibility and regular reviews.

The final performance item to ensure is post-project delivery. It is critical that once the project is complete, the new product or service can be sustained. In the organisational reviews we carry out, from whole-of-organisational level to individual performance level, we see many individuals and organisations thinking they are doing OK, but this does not align with reality. This misinterpretation is a result of operating in an ad-hoc manner, creating an inability to accurately measure performance.

"Ad-hoc" is a simple definition for low-maturity organisations. Their challenge is lack of defined processes, staff either not following the processes and/or not being trained in the processes, and therefore not knowing the cost of failure. If we go with the average failure rate, which is 66% not achieving all their objectives, that means only one-third of strategic goals will be achieved in full. Even if we use the statistic that 33% fail completely, that still means that if you are overseeing a $100m portfolio, about $33m of this investment is going to waste.

The $100m question is, which $33m is going to waste? If you are a low-maturity organisation it will be difficult to answer this question and you will see lots of wasted effort, but not know the full consequences.

We also see many organisations focusing all their measurements on things that have occurred — lag metrics. The challenge here is, an organisation may see there is a problem but will be unable to do anything about it as the event or task is in the past.

To be able to change the course of activities it is critical to have lead indicators that allow you and your team to extrapolate and provide a more accurate prediction of the future. A well-known technique within the project management field is measuring project performance, which can be achieved by defining a value to each set of activities or deliverables and reviewing if the deliverables are taking more or less cost and time to complete. If more, then extrapolating this information to the conclusion of your project will show how much over time or budget it will be at completion.

For the organisation to be successful, you as a high-performing executive must focus on the right activities and help your teams agree on what is achievable, and assign clear metrics to validate the achievement. This approach requires your investment in working on the business, but you will find that once in place your precious hours will be freed up.

Are you ready to start? If so write a list of forward-looking performance metrics that are aligned to your organisational purpose.

[2] en.wikipedia.org/wiki/System_of_systems
[3] hbr.org/2016/01/collaborative-overload
[4] startwithwhy.com/
[5] startwithwhy.com/find-your-why
[6] news.gallup.com/opinion/gallup/216155/reasons-why-employee-engagement-programs-fall-short.aspx
[7] Caliper Profile
[8] www2.deloitte.com/content/dam/Deloitte/global/Documents/About-Deloitte/gx-millenial-survey-2016-exec-summary.pdf
[9] www.caliper.com.au
[10] www.axelos.com/best-practice-solutions/msp/what-is-msp

Chapter VI
WHAT BUSINESS ARE YOU IN?

We are all in the business of solving our customers' problems. I'm sorry, but it may come as a surprise that your customers are not that interested in your products or services or what you actually do. They are in fact coming to you for help solving a problem they have. If they could take a pill or push a button and magically make the problem go away, they probably would. If there were a robot that did the job for a fraction of the price you charged, would your customers keep coming back to you? Probably not.

Do you really know who your customers are and what is the biggest problem they have that you solve?

The days of scattergun or mass advertising are over. No longer can you afford to advertise all over the place in the hope that a small group of potential clients actually find you and are interested in buying what you have to sell. Instead, a different approach is required and a focus on a particular group of people, or niche, you can best serve, from whom you get the best results, and with whom you like to work. They share your values and align with a common purpose. This group of clients is your target market.

A common fear people have is that if they focus on a particular small group, surely they will earn less or even turn away a large amount of work. This simply isn't the case. An old adage in business is that if you try to speak to everyone you say nothing to anyone. Just because you speak specifically to your target market, it doesn't necessarily mean you won't work with people outside your target market.

Take, for example, the specialist sports doctor for knee-related issues. He targets elite professional athletes and those competing in high levels of amateur sport. He focuses specifically on knee-related issues instead of treating the general range of sports injuries. Because he specifically communicates to the market that he is a specialist in knee injuries for elite athletes, he is in fact more in demand. Think about it for a second. If you had a knee problem who would you see to get it fixed? A general sports doctor or someone who treats the knees of top-name athletes?

WHO ARE YOUR TARGET MARKETS AND WHAT ARE THEIR PAIN POINTS?

To work this out first you need to understand your ideal customer. Once you have identified your specific target customer, you can now start to zoom in on their specific pain points and problems. Each specific target market has a unique set of pain points to problems that are either not relevant to, or considered by, a different target market.

To work out their pain points, put yourselves in your customers' shoes and ask yourself these questions:

- what keeps me up at night?
- what frustrates me?
- if I had a magic wand, what one thing would I wish I could change?

Another way is to ring up the customers that you know best and ask them these questions.

Often the answers you get are not the real problem but are in fact the symptoms, so you need to try the "three whys" approach and map out what the real problems are. The three whys for example could be:

- why am I staying awake at night?
- why is that issue a problem?
- why does that happen?

It is only when you get laser-focused on your target and their biggest problems that you can develop a full and remarkable solution that keeps your customers coming back, have them refer people to you, and allow you to put up your prices while turning away work.

WHAT IS THE PURPOSE OF YOUR ORGANISATION?

Economist and academic Theodore Levitt published an important article in Harvard Business Review in 1960. He identified the vision of most organisations was too constricted and they had a narrow understanding of their business. Organisations found they had been missing opportunities that were plain to see once they adopted the wider view. He also went on to identify how many older industries were disrupted and became obsolete because of this narrow vision. He identified organisations such as Royal Dutch Shell needing to rethink its position — it is in the energy business and not just in the petroleum business.

From our experience, the long-term goals within the strategic plan need to align to the high-level purpose of the organisation. As an example, for Australia to be carbon neutral by 2050 the strategic objectives of multiple agencies should align to this goal. It will be interesting to see if this collaboration can occur as government policy directs its agencies to focus on their area and not overlap. On top of this they are often just behind where they would like to be from a task-completed perspective, or they are battling to achieve response times from the minister's office, with fewer staff year on year to do the work. As such, they are challenged to focus on their own needs let alone look outside their silo to support another agency.

When focusing on people, this clarity of purpose is often not the case and when your question (what is your role/job?) is answered, a functional-based response is the norm. These include: "I am a business analyst working on 'project code name'," or "I am a contact centre manager." This tells you a little of what they do, but misses the why. We recommend you ask all staff to adopt the cultural change or ritual of focusing on the intent. People should understand how they contribute to the organisational goals.

Examples of this would be: "I am supporting the organisation open a new market as a business analyst on 'project code name'," or "My team and I have increased our customer retention by 10% as contact centre manager."

If your team are starting with intent, it is more meaningful to you and in fact by doing this it encourages a clear purpose to be defined so they can all align to it. When there are competing purposes, such as taking costs out of a contact centre and reducing customer wait times, the conflict is more obvious and can be worked through to resolution, rather than be unknown and cause issues down the line.

Something we are passionate about is the environment, and working towards a more sustainable future, which is why we say PMLogic is a project management company helping executives deliver their strategic objectives in a sustainable way. The sustainable way refers to the repeatable habits or rituals that form good practice in their organisation as well as the external environment.

Chapter VII
SUSTAINABILITY AND THE SDGs

Sustainability is one of the most diffuse and commonly misunderstood terms. Many people initially think sustainability is solely about the environment or being "green", however there is much more to the term. Sustainability involves each of us doing our part to build the kind of world — economically, environmentally and socially — that we want to live in, and one that we want our children and grandchildren to inherit. At a practical level, this involves each of us being aware of the effect our day-to-day choices have on the intricate balance of social, economic and ecological systems.

Sustainability is often spoken of in terms of "sustainable development". One of the most widely used definitions is that proposed in the World Commission on Environment and Development's Brundtland report, also called "Our Common Future", released in 1987: "... development that meets the needs of the present without compromising the ability of future generations to meet their own needs." While this definition does not specifically make reference to environmental, social and economic measures, these dimensions are implied.

In the corporate world, sustainability has gained traction through social responsibility programs and the adoption of triple bottom line (TBL) accounting. John Elkington, a world authority on corporate responsibility and sustainable development, makes the argument that companies should be leveraging three separate bottom lines. One is the traditional measure of corporate profit, the profit-and-loss account. The second is the bottom line of a company's "people" or "social account", which is a measure of an organisation's social responsibility. The third is the bottom line of the company's "planet" account — a measure of environmental impact. According to Elkington, only a company that produces a TBL is accounting for the full cost involved in doing business.

The difficulty in defining corporate responsibility is touched on by John Campbell, Professor of Sociology at Dartmouth College, and whose research interests span economic and political sociology, comparative political economy, and institutional theory. Campbell believes a company's stakeholders determine its corporate responsibility — that is, all those with an interest in its operations: shareholders, employees, customers, suppliers, regulators, local communities and the environment.

"... we can argue that corporate behaviour is socially responsible as long as it meets [stakeholders'] expectations regarding appropriate and acceptable corporate behaviour." (2007: 950).

Clear purpose simplifies decisions about what to innovate and helps define criteria and metrics to observe and measure innovation, taking into account the environmental, social and economic impacts. There are generally four ways to measure purpose in organisations:

- **Customers** — creating a measure of success based on the positive value that is created for the end user/customer.
- **Employees** — creating a measure of success based on employee well-being and productivity, driven by the creation of meaningful opportunities for them. Paying livable wages, providing quality healthcare and competence development are a few examples
- **Suppliers** — creating a measure of success based on sustainable sourcing, transparency, and serving as an ethical influencer throughout their supply chain.
- **Market** — ccreating and measuring success based on market changes that are linked to the purpose-based innovations an organisation has demonstrated within its sphere of influence.

Note that purpose-driven shouldn't be confused with goal-oriented in that if the organisation lacks purpose, it may have an inherent assumption that its goals are value-creating when they may not be. Rather, it means weaving purpose-driven environmental and social considerations into the fabric of the organisation's operations as well as its goods and services.

SUSTAINABILITY PERSPECTIVES

In a recent McKinsey survey, it was suggested that one potential reason so many companies don't actively address sustainability, despite the attention paid to it by the media and some consumers and investors, is that many have no clear definition of it.

"Unpacking" sustainability into components allows us to gain a far better understanding.

PEOPLE (SOCIETY)

The people or society dimension is focused on a number of elements including labour practices and decent work; society and customers; human rights and ethical behaviour.

In most Western or developed countries, work practices, rates of pay and conditions, worker health and safety, and anti-discrimination is clearly spelt out in legislation or regulations. However, this is not the case in many developing countries where resources and raw materials for products are mined or where products are manufactured or assembled.

Poor labour practices or human rights abuses, such as the use of slave or child labour, occur in some supply chains of large Western multinational firms. This is often without the firms' understanding or knowledge. But in some cases the firms are fully aware of the situation, which calls their business ethics into question.

With the advent of the internet and cameras in mobile phones and devices, and the easy access to large numbers of people through social media, these abuses can go viral and quickly reach millions of people around the world. This has the potential to significantly damage the reputation of organisations and in doing so destroy share value or an organisation's credibility.

PLANET (ENVIRONMENT)

The environment or planet dimension includes elements of transport, energy, water, and waste, and is often the first thing people think of when they hear the word "sustainability". Often these are regulated or legislated, whereby the level of emissions or pollution is either limited to a particular level, or in the case of toxic chemicals, completely prohibited. But it is not just about being "green".

Our consumer-based society operates largely on the model of make/ use/waste, resulting in the consumption of largely non-renewable resources and production of volumes of waste or byproducts, which then need to be disposed of. While recycling has become common, leading companies are moving towards a cradle-to-cradle, or circular economy, whereby waste from one business or process is used as the raw materials for another, thus minimising the volume to be disposed of, and also reducing costs of raw material inputs.

By August of each year, humans have consumed what the planet can regenerate. Between January and July, more carbon is emitted than the forests and oceans can absorb for the entire year. We are over-fishing, over-harvesting, and over-consuming potable water. In all, we consume the natural resources of 1.7 Earths a year.

Earth overshoot day, the day in which we have reached our consumption limit, has been moving closer to January each year. It was first calculated in 1986 as falling in November. In 1993, it moved to October, and in

2017 it was August 2. Some countries exceed their consumption limit much sooner. The UK, for example, reaches its consumption limit by early May. The only country to not exceed its limits is Honduras.

One of the reasons for overconsumption is global population increases. According to the UN Population Fund, there are more than seven billion people in the world, which is twice the amount of 1970 and four-times the amount of 1910. In terms of net gain, we are adding 200,000 people to the planet each day, and according to projections, we are headed to more than nine billion, which is unsustainable.

Over-consumption has impacted our oceans with acidification increasing more than 30% since the beginning of the Industrial Revolution, according to the US National Oceanic and Atmospheric Agency. It is believed the increased acidification levels caused a bleaching of Australia's Great Barrier Reef in 2016 and 2017, the first time it has occurred in back-to-back years. It takes 10 years for the fastest corals to recover, and back-to-back bleaching events offer no opportunity for recovery (Dr James Kerry et al, James Cook University, 2017).

Renewable energy generation through wind turbines, hydroelectric, tidal action or photovoltaic (solar) panels is now commonplace, with large industrial as well as small-scale residential systems being used around the world. Electronic goods manufacturers are focusing on reducing energy consumption in appliances, largely driven by consumer demand and the desire to reduce energy use and save money as a result, given the significant increase in energy costs.

Transportation has also become topical in recent years, with a push towards the increased use of public mass transit systems instead of private cars. The desire to reduce smog drives this, but also the high levels of congestion experienced in many cities. Air travel, in particular, is one of the most highly polluting forms of transport. One of the other major contributors is animal agriculture.

With the advent of broadband internet and applications such as Skype, it is now possible to operate "virtually", and eliminate the need for daily commuting to a city-based office. Phone and video-conferencing allow most activities to be done remotely, and now you can buy "taste" food or meat that hasn't resulted in the death of an animal, so by reducing your meat intake you can do your bit for the environment too.

PROFIT (ECONOMIC OR FINANCIAL)

The profit or economic dimension recognises that for firms to continue to operate over the medium to long term, they need to be profitable. It is only when a firm is profitable that it pays tax, which governments use to support citizens in need and provide health, education and other essential services.

In the case of the P5 standard for sustainability in project management, consideration is also given to business cases for change initiatives and also the need to identify potential opportunities for local economic stimulation through the development of new industries, or providing ongoing cost savings for a community.

There has been recent debate about identifying the true costs of products or services, and in particular, changing the accounting rules to cost in degradation of the environment or specific negative social impacts. This has the potential to create a paradigm shift and if done so could result in a Big Mac costing about $200 — assuming obviously, that it is still made using meat from an animal.

THE STAKEHOLDER VIEW OF THE ORGANISATION

In the modern age of business, transparency has become the new black. When a business, particularly a larger business, lacks transparency, stakeholders get suspicious, because no organisation is completely squeaky clean. Larger organisations also tend to have longer supply chains that often reach into developing countries where environmental, health and safety and employment standards either don't exist or are not at the same level we would expect in the developed world.

With the advent of the internet, access to vast amounts of information about any organisation is readily available. Millions of people carrying mobile phones with cameras can capture images quickly and easily as events happen. These images can be instantly transmitted to hundreds or thousands of people through social media. Twitter, Facebook and the many thousands of review sites provide easy access to stakeholders to post comments and reviews of an organisation. If stakeholders are unhappy, see something that they don't like or have an axe to grind, they can anonymously make their concerns known to large audiences.

Millennials were born in the age of the internet. As global citizens they have a different perspective on the idea of "consumption" and are fully cognisant of sustainability and the potential impacts that our behaviours and actions may have on their future. Millennials are the generation that will face the issues of water shortages, climate change and energy costs that spiral out of control. They do not think twice about posting their views and opinions on social media for all the world to see.

As the level of stakeholder awareness of sustainability issues grow, organisations face an increasing level of responsibility to act ethically and to demonstrate their behaviours are not harming the environment or vulnerable groups in society. But it's not just millennials who have this view. Stakeholders want a clear conscience and greater governance standards to protect customers, suppliers, employees, society and the environment. These changing stakeholder expectations have resulted in a strong push to improve the visibility of what a company does and doesn't do, as demonstrated through its published annual report. This creates a number of unidentified and significant risks for the modern business.

Research by the English *Guardian* newspaper[11] identified a series of non-government organisation campaigns targeting large companies. It found the 10 largest companies by market share in every sector, except finance, attracted 50%-70% of NGO attention. This unwanted attention often resulted in articles on the web and even in the media criticising particular policies, acts or behaviours. It placed a spotlight on what the organisation did, how it did it and also clearly showed where there may have been unacceptable impacts on the environment or society.

So how do you as an executive deal with such issues? Those in the public relations industry may suggest that when the "shit hits the fan", you either say nothing or simply deny it. However, being more proactive ahead of time and engaging with external stakeholders is a far better starting point.

In Australia, near the Great Barrier Reef, there is currently a proposal for a new coal port, Abbot Point, and plans for additional coalmines. If all the coal from the proposed Galilee Basin mines is burned, it will result in an incredible increase in emissions. It has been estimated that it would be 705 million tonnes of CO_2 per year, compared to Australia's total 402 million tonnes in 2010. The other risk of damage is to Australia's tourism industry — nobody flies down under to see a dead reef with limited animals due to the extra noise from the port activity.

The coal port is facing legal challenges from environmental and indigenous groups, and over finance. A number of major banks including Citigroup, Morgan Stanley and Goldman Sachs have said they will not finance the project.

POTENTIAL IMPACTS

McKinsey research shows 70% of company earnings are at risk due to reputation loss. This significant potential loss stems from a number of sources, including impacts in the customer base, financial or valuation, brand and media or in relation to staff. But the impacts are not purely financial. There are a number of key categories of impacts.

Customer base — These impacts largely result in a loss of revenue and a reduction in customer demand, including::

- damage to existing customer relationships
- write-downs in revenues
- loss of existing customers
- inability to form new customer relationships
- decline in demand for an organisation's products or services
- loss of key contracts
- loss of the social licence to operate.

Financial — These impacts often result in a decrease in share value, lead to increased costs, or create challenges in terms of investment. This includes:

- significant fall in share price (listed company)
- withdrawal of donations or donor support (not-for-profit)
- perception of being higher-risk investment
- inability to attract debt and make investments
- paying a higher rate on borrowings
- aggressive takeover by competitor
- increased levels of scrutiny and therefore a high level of compliance due to regulator intervention
- lower valuation.

Brand and media — These impacts focus on the public appearance of the organisation. This may include:

- negative media coverage
- social media backlash
- negative brand perception
- lack of interest in collaboration from current or prospective partners.

Staff — These impacts focus on the ability to attract or retain staff and include:

- inability to recruit
- loss of key staff.

So given these threats and impacts, how do we manage reputation risk?

84% of respondents indicate that the CEO has the major responsibility for managing reputation risk[12].
Economist Intelligence Unit

To mitigate risks, the Australian Centre for Corporate Social Responsibility has identified a number of actions that can be put in place. These are:

- maintaining timely and efficient communications among shareholders, customers, boards of directors, and employees
- establishing strong enterprise risk management policies and procedures throughout the organisation, including an effective anti-fraud program
- creating awareness at all staff levels to reinforce a risk-management culture
- enforcing a code of conduct for the board, management, and staff to instil ethics throughout the organisation

- developing a comprehensive system of internal controls and practices, including those related to computer systems and transactional websites
- complying with current laws and regulations and enforcing existing policies and procedures
- implementing independent testing and transactional testing on a regular basis
- responding promptly and accurately to bank regulators, oversight professionals (such as internal and external auditors), and law enforcement
- establishing a crisis management team in the event there is a significant action that may trigger a negative impact on the organisation.

How many of the above do you have in place?

Given the significant impacts that exist in the supply chain, traceability is required. Traceability is: " ... the ability to identify and trace the history, distribution, application and location of products, parts and materials, to ensure the reliability of sustainability claims, in the areas of human rights (including health and safety), the environment, and anti-corruption."[13]

The Australian Centre for Corporate and Social Responsibility suggest three simple questions be asked in relation to any product your organisation purchases:

- how was this made and where? (Provenance)
- what are the social and environmental impacts of this product right down to source? (Sustainability)

And in relation to the supplier:

- are you telling me everything? (Transparency)

Full traceability of the supply chain for key products is essential if sustainability and reputation risks are to be mitigated. With the top 20 suppliers receiving about 40% of the total supplier spend, on average, this is a great place to start. In addition, more tactical measures can be put in place, including: managing supplier sustainability risks through policies, risk assessments, supplier engagement and collaboration, audit and measurement, leadership and training.

The high-profile supply chain failures of recent times have inflicted heavy reputational damage on some leading global brands, and investors want to insure against such a risk.[14]
Australian Centre for Corporate and Social Responsibility

How will you explain to the board that the risk wasn't assessed and the company reputation could have been saved had it been done sooner?

COST SAVINGS

The desire to save money largely drives many sustainability initiatives. After all, who doesn't like to save money? With rising energy, water and fuel costs, firms are examining the usage and putting in place actions to lower their consumption. Hotels, for example, have actively engaged in the replacement of incandescent light bulbs with low-voltage LED lights, which not only significantly reduce power consumption, but by generating less heat, also reduce the load on artificial cooling systems.

There has also been a move to renewable energy generation, with consumers installing photovoltaic (PV) panels to generate "free" electricity and reduce the need to draw from the electricity grid. Consumers have been incentivised through generous "feed-in" tariffs whereby energy companies pay a multiple of the purchase price for each kilowatt generated, often resulting in no, or a very low, energy bill.

REDUCTION IN MATERIAL USE

Reducing material use and any associated waste means greater resource efficiency, less pollution and more profits. Each dollar saved on raw materials costs goes straight to the bottom line. Raw material costs have edged up over the past few years. Achieving savings through better use of resources has a tangible effect on companies' bottom lines. As such, manufacturers have been actively optimising the use of resources and materials and have used management techniques such as kaizen, and mathematical modelling to minimise material use.

WASTE REDUCTION

The mantra for many years has been reduce, reuse or recycle, with a view to eliminating the levels of waste produced and being either incinerated or sent to landfill. Often valuable and rare elements can be recovered and reused or are able to be incorporated into new products, reducing the levels of raw materials required.

Given the technological age in which we live, however, there are new types of waste being generated at increasing volumes each year.

CHANGING COMMUNITY EXPECTATIONS

As we have noted, with the rise of access to information that can be accessed via the internet, cameras in mobile devices and social media that provides a platform to communicate to millions of people, it is very easy to find out about companies or to post information about a company's actions or perceived violations of regulations. Society is forming an ethical or morally appropriate stance as consumers are becoming more aware of who they buy from.

Community expectations are shifting, with consumers and the public at large being able to call out apparent human rights or environmental concerns and reach a global audience through social media. In response to such expectations, programs such as Fairtrade have been launched. This program publically recognises both individual products and businesses that are working positively to ensure human rights are respected in their supply chain. Other businesses demonstrate their corporate social responsibility through a community investment program, or support charities through financial or in-kind donations.

According to PricewaterhouseCoopers, 87% of consumers in the US believe companies should value the interests of society at least as much as strict business interests. The younger the customer, the more "hooked on green", so this trend isn't likely to abate for a while. It's wise to operate from the assumption that customers will have concerns relating to the environmental impact of your operation and their purchase.[15]

HUMAN RESOURCES CHALLENGES

Attracting talent

A recent survey of more than 3700 students at top business schools showed nearly half would choose a lower salary if it meant working for a company with better environmental environmental practices.

About 20% also said they would not work for a company with poor environmental practices, despite the salary.

Creating buy-in and engaging staff in sustainability

Paul Polman, CEO of Unilever best defines the problem:

"Besides the financial benefits that sustainability practices like energy conservation provide, studies have found that employee retention, productivity, and overall engagement all go up. Nevertheless, it is hard for companies to operationalize sustainability goals, even when the people working for these companies, including their leaders, care about sustainability in the world. The problem is that not enough companies have yet figured out how to link their employees' values and support for sustainability with the employees' daily work and the company's operations. In other words, it's not in the why, but in the how of embedding sustainability where the gap lies."

The recommendation is to form a Green Team to commence this process. Just as a PMO or EPMO should do for projects, a Green Team increases employee engagement and focuses more minds on tackling tough problems and coming up with creative solutions, thereby gaining more buy-in from employees and creating a stronger culture of sustainability.

Polman mentions that Green Teams will often focus on two broad areas. One focus is on the company's own operations — examining the sustainability opportunities within the organisation. The second is on educating employees on sustainability and engaging them in actions they can do at home.

INVESTOR EXPECTATIONS

Banks and other investors are showing increasing levels of interest in the sustainability policies and practices of organisations in which they invest. This is understandable when research (Bergius, 2008) has shown that a company's future business success is linked to its social and environmental performance and that the best-in-class businesses have higher customer retention rates and lower energy, facilities, paper and logistics costs. Laggards, on the other hand, face significantly higher costs. (See also Senxian and Jutras, 2009.)

Investor decision rules are changing

A Morgan Stanley analyst raised the stock price target of three giant apparel companies (Nike, Hanesbrands and VF) based on their management of environmental, social, and governance (ESG) issues.

Market changes

China has reduced demand for coal, recently announcing the list of industries set to be covered by its national carbon market will include petrochemicals, power, construction and steel industries, and even aviation.

The UK government has announced it will decommission coal-fired power plants and aim to be 100% renewable by 2030.

UN SUSTAINABLE DEVELOPMENT GOALS

In 2011, Colombia proposed the adoption of 17 sustainable development goals (SDGs). The UN, together with business leaders, governments, the science community, and others came together in support of the SDGs as the best way to address the sustainability challenges our world faces. This support was affirmed in a resolution from the 2012 RIO+20 Conference, commonly known as "The Future We Want" and a subsequent 2012 report titled "Realizing the Future We Want". Shown below, the SDGs build on the successes of the millennium development goals (MDGs), which expired in January of 2015.

While the SDGs include new areas such as climate change, economic inequality, innovation, sustainable consumption, peace, and justice, the goals are interconnected so that success on one goal contributes to the success of another. These goals are the single greatest project that humanity as a collective has undertaken.

There is a vast amount of information about the SDGs on the web and in the public domain. Organisations and individuals who influence trades and professions should support the goals and contextualise them for their industry. The goals and targets will stimulate action over the next 15 years in areas of critical importance for humanity and the planet (UN, 2017):

United Nations Sustainable Development Goals (SDGs)

- **People** — to end poverty and hunger, in all their forms and dimensions, and to ensure that all human beings can fulfill their potential in dignity and equality and in a healthy environment.
- **Planet** — to protect the planet from degradation, including through sustainable consumption and production, sustainably managing its natural resources and taking urgent action on climate change, so that the planet can support the needs of the present and future generations.
- **Prosperity** — to ensure that all human beings can enjoy prosperous and fulfilling lives and that economic, social, and technological progress occurs in harmony with nature.
- **Peace** — to foster peaceful, just, and inclusive societies that are free from fear and violence. There can be no sustainable development without peace and no peace without sustainable development.

- **Partnership** — to mobilise the means required to implement this agenda through a revitalised Global Partnership for Sustainable Development, based on a spirit of strengthened global solidarity, focused in particular on the needs of the poorest and most vulnerable, and with the participation of all countries, all stakeholders, and all people.

The interlinkages and integrated nature of the Sustainable Development Goals are of crucial importance in ensuring they are achieved. And if they are achieved, the lives of all will be profoundly improved, and the world will be transformed for the better.

For more information, visit **sustainabledevelopment.un.org/sdgs**

[11] www.theguardian.com/sustainable-business/2015/feb/09/corporate-ngo-campaign-environment-climate-change

[12] Economist Intelligence Unit http://www.acegroup.com/eu-en/assets/risk-reputation-report.pdf

[13] A Guide to Traceability - A Practical Approach to Advance Sustainability in Global Supply Chains". UN Global Compact, 2014

[14] ACCSR Whitepaper: First five steps to a sustainable supply chain

[15] playbook.amanet.org/what-is-customer-service-6-major-trends-changing-the-customers-expectations/

Chapter VIII

THE DIFFICULTY OF EXECUTING STRATEGY

Strategic management theorists have suggested an organisation does not and cannot exist as a self-contained island, isolated from its environment.

The environment in which businesses operate is changing dramatically. Population growth, advances in technology, and shifts in society and employment arrangements make the world in which we live and work immeasurably different to what it was 20 years ago.

Disruptive events, scandals, crises and shocks constantly take executives by surprise. Senior executive leadership transitions suddenly change the outlook of specific strategies or even product or service offerings that have taken months or years to develop. Executives are constantly required to work collaboratively across internal and external boundaries, engage a wide and often conflicting network of stakeholders, and recruit and manage an increasingly diverse and independently minded workforce. And nothing ever stands still. Then there is the added pressure to be "innovative" and experiment with new policy and program ideas in a context of risk-averse shareholders.

Many of these changes are driven by megatrends.

MEGATRENDS

Futurist Richard Watson has identified a series of trends that allow him to create an image of the world awaiting us. These trends identify the issues associated with society, technology, energy, the environment, the economy, employment, population, politics and identity. In addition, Watson identifies seven megatrends that are all-encompassing, many of which present a series of fundamental challenges to businesses and have the potential to wipe out organisations that don't adapt and deal with the disruption they are likely to cause. We will now examine each of these in turn.

GLOBALISATION AND DEREGULATION

We now live in a global marketplace that operates around the clock. It is very rare that products we use do not contain components sourced from overseas or are manufactured or assembled in another country. The labour market is much the same. Through the advent of the internet, workers can be sourced offshore from lower-cost economies, which in turn can either improve profitability or technical expertise. It is now common for virtual teams to deliver projects around the clock.

This is evident in the airline industry, where Boeing for example sources parts for the 787 Dreamliner from China, South Korea, Australia, Japan, the United States, Canada, England, France, Sweden and Italy. And this is for external components alone.

Globalisation is great if we are buying cheaper electronics or televisions, but it's not so great when we see well-paid workers losing their jobs to offshore companies operating in low-cost economies such as India or The Philippines, or full-time permanent positions give way to freelancing and the gig economy. People now find project-based work through apps such as Upwork and Freelancer instead of applying for jobs in the newspaper or online. Work itself is also being redefined, with individuals searching for not just a job, but a role that gives them purpose and meaning in their lives.

To remain competitive in this global market, governments — apart from the US and China — are removing tariffs and trade barriers, pursuing free-trade agreements with larger economies intended to boost export sales and jobs in the smaller economy. The size of government and the level of taxation levied is a regular discussion in the media, and deregulation and reduction of "red tape" are put forward as ways to improve productivity and in turn generate tax revenue.

URBANISATION AND MIGRATION

By 2050, about 70% of the world's population will live in urban areas. While this more concentrated and centralised population has advantages, it also creates pressure on housing, city infrastructure, employment, and creates traffic congestion. As a result, significant investments in new infrastructure are required.

Along with urbanisation we are experiencing an increase in wealth, an improved standard of living, and a demand for consumer products. Everyone, it seems, wants the latest Samsung Galaxy or Apple iPhone.

CLIMATE CHANGE AND SUSTAINABILITY

Despite the Paris Agreement on Climate Change, the world continues to face increasing greenhouse gas emissions. And while many countries have already publicly announced the shutdown of fossil fuel electricity generation, the emerging middle class and massive urbanisation continues to create demand for cheap energy.

Governments in countries such as Australia face a challenge. We are home to one of the world's largest coal reserves, yet if we are to meet our commitment to the Paris Agreement, most of that coal needs to remain in the ground. Politically, the introduction of carbon pricing has proven to be difficult, particularly in Australia, due in part to gamesmanship of conservative politicians and also to the country's almost total reliance of coal for electricity and thousands of blue-collar jobs over the past 200 years.

Sea levels will rise, extreme weather events will multiply, and water sources and agricultural production will be less reliable.

Climate change has significant impacts on food production. Starbucks' biggest risk is its ability to source high-quality coffee beans. Climate change is rapidly changing growing conditions, which affects the ability of producers to provide the high-quality beans Starbucks expects.

And if you are concerned about coffee, you can also spare a thought for chocolate. If the world's temperature increases by 2.3°C by 2050, then smallholders in Ghana and Côte d'Ivoire, many of whom are Fairtrade certified and produce more than half of the world's chocolate,[16] are also going to find it very difficult to grow cocoa pods.

POPULATION AND LIFESPAN GROWTH

The United Nations Population Division predicts a 32% increase in the world's population by 2050, with a predicted 115% increase in Africa, 48% growth in Oceania and a 20% increase in Asia.

Not only is the population growing, but it is also ageing. Workplaces of the future will be very different and there will be significantly fewer people in the workforce supporting a much larger number of retirees. When combined with improvements in medicine and health, it means retirees will also live for much longer and may exhaust their superannuation savings or pension funds, putting increased pressure on the public purse.

Technology will help us live longer and be healthier. Already we are seeing the emergence of transhumanism, with high-tech prosthetics containing dozens of computers, motors and actuators, making limbs incredibly life-like. We are also entering the age of personalised medicine where prescriptions and treatments will be based on an individual's DNA and customised to the specific circumstances. With luck, we are on the verge of curing most, if not all forms of cancer, such that it will only take a course of tablets or the application of a lotion to treat this insidious disease.

We have also already seen developments in 3D printing whereby organic material is able to be duplicated, making mass production of organs and body parts a possibility. Organ donation and people dying waiting for transplants or donors will soon be a thing of the past.

LOCALISM AND RE-REGULATION

In response to job losses, and the other downsides of globalisation, political parties have attempted to tap into the vein of voting public sentiment. "Joe Citizen" is concerned about the increasing cost of living, low-wage growth, big increases in electricity costs and job certainty. Blue-collar industries such as auto manufacturing have shut down and there have been widespread redundancies across many sectors at the same time as governments sign up to a range of international agreements that restrict business actions or require structural change in certain industry sectors.

The more the world becomes global and homogenised the more cultural identity comes to the fore. We saw this with Brexit, where identity trumped economics. We saw it slightly with the election of US President Donald Trump too, where the threat of rising powers and the fear of disappearing influence and employment turned a nation inwards and backwards.[17]

Some commentators say these megatrends create an increasingly complicated world, which leads to an increase in volatility, uncertainty, complexity and ambiguity, or VUCA[18].

WHAT IS VUCA?

The US Army War College introduced the concept of VUCA in the 1990s and business leaders have adopted it to describe a chaotic, turbulent and rapidly changing environment.

Volatility

Volatility relates to the nature, speed, volume, magnitude and dynamics of change. The changes occur rapidly, are unexpected, and have an unclear duration. While the changes themselves are relatively easy to understand, organisations struggle to keep up with the pace of change. This may be due to a level of risk aversion, or perhaps just a response comes too slow.

Uncertainty

Uncertainty is the lack of predictability of issues and events. We do not know what will happen and what the future will be, and as such, surprises are likely. Often organisations tend to resort to what has worked in the past, however this does not deliver the outcome needed.

Complexity

Complexity is the confounding of issues and the chaos that surrounds any organisation. There are too many moving and interconnected parts with unclear causes, effects and interactions, which create an overwhelming amount of information. This tends to lead to:

- analysis paralysis, as organisations attempt to understand the mountain of information
- attempts to address the symptoms rather than the root causes
- short-term, quick wins rather than concentrating on the issues that create sustainable, long-term success.

Ambiguity

Ambiguity is the haziness of reality and the mixed meanings of conditions. There are a multitude of different perspectives and viewpoints with often no precedents. Often events and situations are misinterpreted or the significance of those events are not understood, resulting in managers and executives not taking appropriate actions.

LEADING IN THE AGE OF VUCA

VUCA isn't something to be solved; it simply is. While VUCA creates fragile organisations, attempts to simplify complexity, or attempts to decode and counter volatility, uncertainty, complexity or ambiguity will not make them go away. VUCA can't be mastered through industrial-age structures, practices and thinking.

In the age of VUCA, traditional management methods are no longer sufficient to address the entrepreneurial skills needed to adapt to the volume and rate of change that is occurring. When the environment is unstable and rapidly changing, plans cannot be relied upon and events can arise at rates faster than for which it is practical to re-plan. The classic techniques of control systems, financial forecasting, strategic planning, hierarchical structures and statistical decision making cannot deal with the amount of flux in the environment.

Constant change creates anxiety and can set people on edge because we humans crave certainty. People worry about change affecting their jobs, status, and influence. This can hurt engagement, productivity, and the willingness to act independently. A typical reaction is to address the symptoms by regularly reorganising the business hierarchy and redefining business processes and job roles. But this does not address the root cause, and creates the unintended consequences of change fatigue and chaos. People become confused adapting to new ways, resist them and resort to the way they have always done it, or just simply give up.

We have a framework for thriving in the age of VUCA. We propose a flexible, project-based structure complemented by skills such as teaming that create fluidity and the expectation that structures will evolve. We take into account the role of leadership in this new world and the need to communicate a clear purpose and vision for the organisation, and the modern executive's need for in-depth understanding of their organisation's capabilities to take advantage of rapidly changing circumstances. Agility is critical because strategic adjustments must be made continually.

[16] www.ciatnews.cgiar.org/2011/09/28/too-hot-for-chocolate
[17] toptrends.nowandnext.com/2016/12/19/2017-trends-2
[18] en.wikipedia.org/wiki/Volatility,_uncertainty,_complexity_and_ambiguity

Chapter IX

DEVELOPING AN ADAPTIVE STRATEGY

One key challenge we come across time and time again is the non-alignment of an organisation's strategic plan with the work its people are doing. Or worse, the people are doing work aligned to the strategic plan, which they know is the wrong type of work, but they are being measured against it so feel they have no choice. In both scenarios and from our experience we have found strategic plans cannot be monolithic and static documents. For a strategic plan to continue to represent an organisation's needs it must be adaptable and be developed with delivery in mind. The strategic planning process is often carried out by team members who do not have delivery experience and when organisations use strategy consultants they too are missing the critical knowledge and experience of delivery.

We have also found that executives are not taught sufficient project management or strategy implementation skills in their executive training courses and many of the masters courses are also missing this critical element.

It is not just at the strategy level where there are issues. Project management concepts are shown to be based on approaches to planning that top managers had rejected after 30 years of unsuccessful experience. Persistently high project failure rates and recent developments at the board level suggest we might have reached the limits of our current approaches, and a new approach of developing adaptive strategies that link to an agile delivery model is needed.

In particular, this model needs a different level of focus between top managers and project managers. There is unfortunately limited research into the overlap between strategy in the management literature and projects to implement strategy. We draw on our personal experience of establishing strategy implementation methodologies and using these to improve the delivery of programs and projects to provide some evidence of how a new focus could work.

The use of projects to implement strategy is a much newer development because projects have been traditionally associated with new product development (Artto, et al 2008). Projects began to be understood as a means to implement strategy and change in the 1970s in the strategic management literature and in the late-1980s in the project management literature. Further tentative developments in our understanding of strategy in the project management literature occurred with the developments of program management, portfolio management and enterprise-wide approaches to project management.

A seminal 1994 publication may explain why research into strategy implementation has not made much progress. Mintzberg's 1994 article "The rise and fall of strategic planning" described the failure of strategic planning to produce the expected results despite decades of intensive effort. With the decline of strategic planning, its teams and three-to-five-year long-range plans, strategists had to focus on finding and developing new approaches. These include Porter's five forces model, generic strategies, the resource-based view of the firm, and dynamic capabilities. Mintzberg and Waters (1985) suggested that disruptive change had rendered ineffective the analysis of past trends as a technique to predict and plan for the future. As a result, firms have steered away from deliberate and planned approaches, and relied instead on patterns of strategy to emerge over time. Often these patterns are only identified in hindsight — looking backwards at what an organisation has done.

The modern business environment is turbulent and has been rocked by unpredictable forces such as deregulation, globalisation, technological discontinuities and environmental concerns (Prahalad & Hamel 1994; Emery & Trist 1963). Customer tastes change more rapidly than the quarterly or annual planning cycles, as do the demands of other key stakeholders such as investors and suppliers. Most recently, the effects of the ageing population have introduced another seismic issue related to staff and skill shortages. The relatively stable and static world that preceded the Industrial Revolution no longer exists. These considerations suggest the environment in which the optimal portfolio operates is not static, but ever-changing because the strategies and priorities of an organisation need to react to the market and external environmental shocks. The rational, mechanistic underpinnings of portfolio management may therefore be unsuited to meet these demands.

STRATEGY IMPLEMENTATION

In contrast, program management adapts to change and is a tool for strategy implementation (Artto et al 2008). Its main strength is the recognition that programs, rather than individual projects, are generally needed to realise strategic goals. In theory, to respond to changes, projects can be added to or dropped from a program as required. However, program management is far from being a mature discipline (Stretton 1992).

The literature is sparse with very few published texts (Williams & Parr 2004; PMI 2008; Reiss et al 2006; Milosevic, Martinelli & Waddell 2007; OGC 2007; Thiry 2010) and only one with a strategic orientation (Pelligrinelli 2008). Curiously, all these texts start by commenting on the dearth of available guidance. Milosevic et al (2007) explain that program management originated in the US aerospace and defence industries where it was kept secret for decades. They add that it was only in the 1980s that program management took hold in the commercial sector and even then, it was sometimes just the term being misapplied by project managers to the management of large or multiple projects.

The strategic orientation of program management is seen in the leading methodology, Managing Successful Programs, which focuses on the delivery of change (OGC 2007). The only other well-known methodology, Standard for Program Management, is more project-oriented and focuses on new product development (PMI 2006).

Some have argued these mainstream program-management methodologies are too strongly influenced by the rational project-management tradition because practices have been codified too rigidly (Lycett, Rassau & Danson 2004). Pellegrinelli et al (1997) find the required level of documentation works against the need to challenge and redefine the program as new information comes to hand. They believe current guidelines understate the need to adapt to the strategic context and ensure the strategic benefits are actually realised. The mainstream approaches are focused on a narrowly defined program and assign responsibility for the realisation of benefits to business managers at the boundaries of the program (OGC 2009). Pellegrinelli et al (2007) conclude the current codification into a common set of transferable principles and processes is inadequate and report that practitioners have found many of the guidelines are either not useful or do not make sense.

The literature also has another related concept: project strategy. Project strategy mirrors the bottom-up concept of alignment. Project strategy is the direction or approach taken in a project to ensure it makes the greatest contribution to success in its environment (Artto et al 2008). Project strategy relates to the way the project team sets about achieving a project's objectives and goals (Dinsmore and Cooke-Davies 2006). The concept appears to have been developed as a conceptual bridge that links corporate and business unit strategy to the delivery of projects (Morris & Jamieson 2005). Project strategy is typically developed at the start, to agree on goals, and to provide guidelines to execute the work (Artto et al 2008).

THE MINTZBERG PLANNING SCHOOLS

As noted in Chapter III Henry Mintzberg is a Canadian academic and author on business and management. He is currently the Cleghorn Professor of Management Studies at the Desautels Faculty of Management of McGill University in Montreal, Quebec, where he has been teaching since 1968. Three of the Mintzberg schools — planning, learning and positioning — have at various times dominated strategic thought (Mintzberg 1994) and have very close associations with the disciplines of project, program and portfolio management.

PLANNING SCHOOL

The planning school is a prescriptive view of strategy and represents the first and most influential school. It is focused on the process of formulating a strategy rather than the content of the strategy itself. Planning is forward-looking and requires clear articulation of intentions supported by formal controls to ensure plans are consistently pursued in an ever-changing environment (Mintzberg & Waters 1985). It is typified by Ansoff's Model of Strategic Planning where a series of plans are developed at the corporate, business unit and functional level of an organisation and builds on the concepts proposed by Taylor, Fayol, Gilbreth and Gantt. Typically, strategic plans were developed for the medium-to-long term, covering a period of three to five years. The following diagram shows an example where a strategic plan cascades down to operations and projects with alignment between strategy and projects (Stewart 1963).

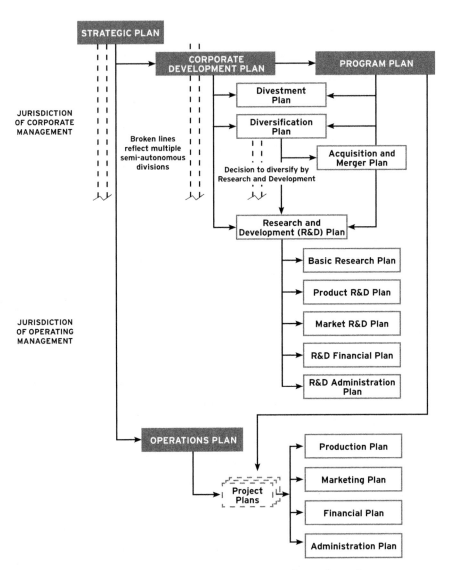

Systems of plans. *Adapted from source: Mintzberg (1994)*

The process of strategic planning starts with specific planning staff formulating a plan and top management approving it. The plans are then decomposed so that lower-level tasks can be scheduled and allocated to specialised areas of the organisation. The strategy is then implemented by operational staff, often in complete isolation from those who formulated or approved the strategy. This approach to strategic planning closely parallels the mainstream project management planning process.

The strategic planning school, however, began to lose favour in the 1980s (Mintzberg, Ahlstrand, & Lampel 2005). The regimented strategic planning process failed to develop any true strategic choices and produced virtually no results (Wilson 1994). Formal plans that were produced either decayed or required constant adjustment during periods of turbulent environmental change: some changes occurring so rapidly that the organisation focused all its efforts on constantly replanning, with strategy implementation never actually occurring (Wilson 1994).

The key reason for the demise of the planning school was the misguided assumption that a formal plan could provide long-term guidance (Wilson 1994). Planners did not entertain the possibility that the environment could not be predicted with any great accuracy (Mintzberg & Waters 1985) and that the plan would be of no use because it could neither be implemented nor be useful even if it were implemented. With rapid change, the process had to be simplified, and well-thought-out strategic plans became nothing more than an extrapolation of existing patterns, or were copied from standard industry recipes (Grinyer & Spencer 1979). In addition, after plans were developed and championed, changes to plans were resisted by top managers in an attempt to save face (Mintzberg & Waters 1985). This dysfunctional behaviour accelerated the downward spiral of planning.

This challenge happens in commercial and government settings, and many reviews have been undertaken including a longitudinal assessment by our colleague, Dr Raymond Young[19] for the NSW State Government in Australia. This review found no evidence to suggest any strategic goals had improved, despite very aggressive project investment ($100 billion) over a 10-year period. Even worse, a similar review was undertaken for the Victorian state government in Australia with the same findings.

Instead of taking a long-range planning approach, we need to be more adaptable and agile.

[19] Young R; Grant J, 2015, 'Is strategy implemented by projects? Disturbing evidence in the State of NSW', International Journal of Project Management, vol. 33, pp. 15 - 28, 10.1016/j.ijproman.2014.03.010

Chapter X
ADAPTABLE AND AGILE IMPLEMENTATION

We live in a world that is more connected than ever before. Back in late-2014 the quantity of mobile devices exceeded the number of people on the planet and with humans multiplying at roughly one person every 16 seconds, that is ~1% per year. Mobiles are increasing at 4.7% per year. With the high quantity of different devices and mobiles, it is critical that global standards are set and mobile devices adhere to these standards, otherwise they are not compatible. There are some famous examples where different organisations developed two standards, such as Betamax and VHS, and only the VHS survived — for a while that is, before hard-disc recorders replaced them.

This demand for connectedness and the multiplicity of standards increases complexity and therefore predictability of outcome. The half-life of devices also increases the requirement of a continued investment just to remain current. All of these changes mean static strategic goals based on defined outputs is becoming an obsolete approach to measuring performance, with the latest approach being outcome-based goals that are low on specification, and likely to change.

An agile approach to delivering your strategic goals is critical to success. When we say agile, we don't mean you have to get your whole organisation trained in one of the Agile software or project management methods; we mean the agile philosophy of allowing changes to your initiatives is critical.

Gone are the days when you could set up a scope of work that did not change, and once delivered, the team claimed the project as a huge success. There are many examples of this approach where the project was delivered to time, cost and scope but the outcomes and expected benefits were not achieved.

To resolve this issue, we recommend the strategy is made up of fixed and variable elements. If the strategy is set over a five-year period, then the macro and short-term goals to be achieved over the whole period should be static and the medium term should be adjustable. That way your organisation is able to adjust to the changing environment within which it is operating. To enable these adjustments to take place we recommend a quarterly review and update of the strategic plan. This review should help you confirm you are on track to deliver the long-term strategic objectives, that you have achieved the strategic objectives for the previous period, and enable you to refine the medium-term objectives.

Having a bi-modal approach to delivering your strategic objectives will improve the speed of delivery and reduce bureaucracy fatigue where delivery teams are forced into following a method that does not fit the work they are wishing to complete. This not only reduces the likelihood of them successfully completing, but also means a lot of time is spent developing documents and reporting on items that do not help you or your fellow executives gain confidence that the strategic objective will be achieved.

We have developed a delivery model that achieves this and have learnt that the strategic goals also need to be validated on a regular basis. We would recommend quarterly, otherwise the delivery system becomes tangled in meeting emerging needs, as well as meeting objectives within a five-year-old strategic plan that may not be valid.

This approach will only work where there is a separation of goals owned at the executive level and your organisation's teams' delivery, including external partners. This is especially critical within government organisations, where ministers' offices are then able to focus on ensuring the activities within the government agencies are aligned with achieving their high-level goals, rather than getting involved in detailed delivery decisions at the expense of focusing on these high-level goals.

Having this approach will also assist you adopting a more innovative delivery approach, as there is a likelihood that some of the innovative ideas do not succeed. This upsets less-mature organisations because they typically have a culture of expecting everything to succeed. The Standish Group[20] findings over the past 20 years obviously state otherwise and part of helping your organisation to be more successful in delivering its strategic goals will be to provide evidence that your team are not able to reject.

There are many innovation-based approaches you can use from Design Thinking to more complex methodologies. The two methods we regularly use come from Stanford D-School[21] and IDEO[22]. The key benefit you will find in adopting a Design Thinking approach is the engagement of your customers' needs in defining the solution.

Detailed information can be found in each of the approaches, so in summary, rather than starting with a list of requirements or worse, solutions looking for problems to solve, you empathise with them and find out what they need. The key here is asking why, so you get to the root cause. This is similar to the five whys[23] or brainstorming[24] techniques all designed to gain that deeper understanding of your subject.

GAINING CUSTOMER INSIGHTS

The mistakes we see with this approach are not involving your customers, so what you build is based on an interpretation rather than real needs. However, when gaining these needs be careful the innovative solutions are tested regularly. It brings to mind the famous quote from Henry Ford, reprised in an HBR article[25]. When questioned if he believed in asking customers what they wanted, Ford replied: "If I had asked them what they had wanted, they would have said a faster horse." Ford of course was the American inventor and engineer who founded Ford Motor Company, including the process of mass production. He raises an interesting point: sometimes people don't know what they want. As the HBR article notes, Ford's original vision of disproving his potential "customers want faster horses" could have potentially been refined to a vision of "better cars, with better financing options".

Despite making car travel possible for the masses Ford's early lack of adaptability significantly impacted his company and he lost much market share until he responded. Had Ford initiated an adaptable strategy perhaps General Motors would not be the company it is today.

Another approach to gaining input from your customers is through simulations. In the construction industry, 3D modelling has been around for a while and now with BIM[26], buildings, bridges, tunnels and other infrastructure can be fully modelled before any actual construction starts. This has allowed the teams to solve many issues before they arise and if they keep the BIM model up to date they are able to more easily modify what they have built, for example high-rise buildings when there is a change in fire regulations.

The use of BIM takes into account system thinking, as the models can be used, for example, by the fire department for the layout, fire exits and water supply, which reduces the risks emergency service crews face if entering a building on fire.

Our experience with establishing strategic plans, is the long-term goals need to align to the high-level purpose of the organisation. As an example, for Australia to be carbon neutral by 2050 the strategic objectives of multiple agencies should align to this goal. We recommend evaluating the activities being undertaken by the agency to ensure they are supporting this long-term goal. This could be investing in renewable energy, setting a national standard to assess energy usage, and educating those involved in constructing, running and selling items such as buildings and transport in the value of other products with a higher rating.

A holistic approach to thinking about achieving the strategic objectives, such as including the education work outlined above, is critical. This holistic approach must include external factors such as trends and sentiments. It is a mistake to ignore these as they are likely to impact on your strategic plan. An example is an organisation wishing to outsource its IT. If the IT section is not well run, the organisation is in fact just outsourcing a problem, which is then compounded by the fact that it takes a different type of skill, such as strong contract management, to manage a third-party partner or company. This increases the cost as it is not needed if work is done internally.

To reduce the negative impact of these decisions, we recommend you assess the maturity of your organisation's ability to deliver the strategic objectives. This assessment will help identify the least-mature areas. It will also help you compare to other similar organisations if you follow the global best practice Portfolio Programme Project Management Maturity (P3M3®) model. And most importantly, it will help you assess the gaps between your current maturity and the target state you need to achieve for delivery of the objectives within the strategic plan.

The approach to including this delivery assessment in strategic planning is a new one, but we see it is a critical element. A beautifully crafted strategic plan that doesn't take into account the organisational ability to achieve it, is unlikely to garner the required results.

Does your strategic plan have a delivery focus?

An added benefit of undertaking a maturity review of your organisation when developing your strategic objectives is that it engages your delivery teams and helps gain their ideas, input and buy-in into the strategic plan. The input and questions they ask will greatly assist with these teams' understanding of their position and purpose, meaning they are more likely to make informed decisions when it comes to resolving issues and deciding on changes to the programs and projects being run to achieve the strategic objectives.

These delivery teams will also be able to provide the metrics that will help not only confirm that the strategic objectives have been achieved, but with some effort develop lead-based indicators that assist with evaluating that the activities being undertaken are in fact supporting the achievement of the objectives. Their involvement will also help with interdependency management. By modelling the critical chain from what is being developed to the strategic objectives, they are able to assess the dependencies and any gaps/overlaps in their plans.

We specifically call out lead indicators because our research shows their use is disproportionately low compared to lag indicators. We think this is due to lag indicators, such as cost to date, being far easier to define and measure. But it is like navigating a car based on looking through the rear-view mirror to see where you have been, and at best studying a map, the fuel level and speed, rather than looking through the front window to assess the current environment and having your car's map system set up to redirect you based on the most effective way to achieving the destination you desire.

When thinking about navigating, pre-map software was often a source of frustration. One critical item is ownership. If someone is nominated the responsibility to be the navigator and they seek advice and guidance from others, but it is agreed that they are the ultimate decision maker, then there may be disagreement but fewer arguments.

In our view it is the same for your organisation as you and your team navigate the path to achieving all elements of the strategic plan. Our view on how to achieve this is to assign a business owner as a "navigator" for each of your strategic objectives. Your business owner is the ultimate decision maker, and picking up on our previous example, although they may be an expert driver, the role they are being measured against in this case is their ability to navigate in the most effective way to achieve the strategic objective.

The business-owner role is more and more important as the operating environment becomes more volatile, uncertain, complex and ambiguous. It is therefore critical that one of your teams with good knowledge achieving the strategic objectives takes accountability for the activities to deliver it.

With multiple business owners responsible for different strategic objectives, they are able to be the voice for this objective and present to you their respective teams' strengths, weaknesses, opportunities and threats to their achievements. This approach will help with cross-group/divisional/business unit activities, supporting a matrix-based organisational approach, and setting performance-based measures for staff aligned to breaking down your organisational silos.

Interestingly, the average tenure of a CEO in an Australian publicly listed company is five-and-a-half years[27]. We believe this allows time for the CEO to review the organisation, assess what is working and what needs to change, go through a strategic planning cycle, then, like their predecessors, fail to deliver most of their projects and leave before this impacts long term.

Interestingly in Australia there is a trend to hire the CEO from the internal pool and this appears to be working as the longevity of tenure is higher than the global average of 5.3 years, and there is a direct correlation with tenure and long-term results.

We also see organisations such as Macquarie Bank putting the majority of its executives' remuneration against longer-term customer-oriented targets, and its executives only receive these bonuses if they are still working for Macquarie Bank at the time of assessment. This obviously drives a longer-term focused behaviour as well as better retention for executives who do not wish to miss out on their bonuses by leaving.

[20] www.standishgroup.com/outline
[21] dschool.stanford.edu/resources/
[22] www.designkit.org/resources
[23] en.wikipedia.org/wiki/5_Whys
[24] en.wikipedia.org/wiki/Brainstorming
[25] hbr.org/2011/08/henry-ford-never-said-the-fast
[26] en.wikipedia.org/wiki/Building_information_modeling
[27] www.afr.com/leadership/ceo-tenure-hits-fiveyear-high-pwc-finds-20161204-gt3wmy

Chapter XI

CREATING A PROGRAM LOGIC

Central to the process of creating a program logic is structuring a series of initiatives to deliver strategic goals. The program of action is based on a sound theory, which relates changes in the target group behaviour to the achievement of desired end-state objectives. Program logic is a top-down approach that ensures all funded and resourced initiatives contribute towards the achievement of the goals and the delivery of the desired outcomes and benefits, rather than just having some form of superficial alignment.

WHAT IS A PROGRAM?

A program is a collection of projects or initiatives that are grouped together to either achieve economies of scale and efficiencies, or are a series of related initiatives that collectively deliver a strategic outcome, or deliver a specific benefit to the organisation.

In many organisations the strategic plan is nothing more than a nice set of goals or objectives, or perhaps even a colourful poster containing a number of key themes and strategic pillars. To be successful in strategy implementation you need to break the activities down into a series of projects or initiatives. They will enable, contribute to, or deliver against one or more of the organisation's strategic objectives. This new collection of activities and/or products and services should be managed as a program.

To determine whether each project or initiative delivers or enables the organisation's strategy, we need to create a program logic. Program Logic links the initiative being delivered to its activities output, and links projects to outcomes.

OUTCOME HIERARCHY	DEFINITION OF LEVEL
Broader goal	Broader goal if the program links to external commitments (for example, corporate social responsibility). This may have several programs, with different organisations contributing to them. Specifies the broader PESTLEC (political, economic, social, technological, legal, environmental and commercial) goal the program is working towards.
End of program outcome	Desired end result of the program. This can occur some time (several years) after the program has finished. The impact of the program can be on one or more PESTLEC factors. The benefit should be able to be specified in tangible (measurable) terms to validate the commitment of resources.
Intermediate outcome	The changes in individual and group knowledge, skills, attitudes, aspirations, intentions, practices and behaviours.
Immediate outcome	The instant change that occurs as a direct result of the outputs and activities of the program. Generally it includes the levels and nature of awareness, engagement and participation.
Outputs	The results, products and/or services the program will create.
Activities	The actions that will be completed to address the problem, contained within project/business plans.

Table 1 Program Logic elements

They are visual models that map the relationships between inputs and the activities/resources of a program to the changes/goals. These relationships and the pathways are also referred to as theory of change or logic models.

WHY CREATE A PROGRAM LOGIC?

Often the relationships between resources, activities and outcomes (Lawton et al 2014) is not defined and causes misunderstanding and miscommunication between the teams undertaking the activities and the goals the organisation wishes to achieve.

The team should develop the program logic during the planning phase, helping them co-create the activities and outputs needed to achieve the outcomes and goals. It is also a key input in developing the evaluation plan, making it easier to define what evaluation questions you should be asking at what stage of the program.

The program logic should be a "living document" and regularly reviewed, and all but the final program outcome or goal updated to represent the most effective and efficient way to deliver this goal.

HOW DO YOU DEVELOP A PROGRAM LOGIC?

The most effective approach is to start with the end in mind, the goal of your program, and then work backwards through the short and medium-term outcomes or stepping stones to get there and the activities and outputs required to achieve them.

Once you and your team have the program stepping stones, from activities through outputs to outcomes and your ultimate goal in place, you must capture the assumptions and external dependencies. These should be captured as project risks that must be assessed and appropriately treated to ensure they do not prevent you from achieving your goals.

The program logic has four key elements: inputs, activities, outputs and outcomes. The outcomes should be defined as short, medium or long-term.

PROBLEM STATEMENT

What issue or problem is achieving the goal of your program going to solve?

Things to consider are:

- what is the issue/problem?
- what causes the problem and what causes these issues?
- who is impacted by this problem?
- who else cares about solving the problem? And is anyone else is working on solving it?
- what does any research or evidence tell us about the problem?
- what is our collective view and experience of this issue?

(adapted from Shakman and Rodriguez, 2015)

SHORT-TERM OUTCOMES

The short-term or immediate outcomes are typically skills or knowledge-based changes you expect to see on completion of the initial phase of your program. These changes can be thought of as the foundation-level skills and knowledge needed to deliver the program's final outcome or goal. These changes are a "means to an end" and often difficult to justify in isolation. Without the link to the program's goal they are often a negative return on investment (RoI) as they consume more value of resources to create than the value created.

MEDIUM-TERM OUTCOMES

Medium-term or intermediate outcomes are what you should expect to achieve based on having the short-term outcomes in place. So if you have identified an increase in staff or customer knowledge as a short-term outcome, the medium-term outcome is likely to be the application of that knowledge, for example a change in your staff's behaviour in the way they work with each other, deal with customers and a change in the way your customers work with the services your organisation provides.

LONG-TERM OUTCOMES

The long-term or impact outcomes are typically 10 to 30 years or more and should resolve the problems or issues identified in your problem statement. It is important to note that achieving the long-term goal and solving the problems and issues you have identified will be influenced by many factors outside of your control and therefore you must ensure you use an adaptive management approach such as the AgileSHIFT(R) method I have been involved in developing with Axelos, the UK government's commercial arm.
(See www.axelos.com/best-practice-solutions/agile-shift/what-is-agile-shift)

INPUTS

The inputs are you, your team and your customers and non-people resources, such as buildings, equipment, that you are able to draw on to address the issues and problems.

OUTPUTS: ACTIVITIES

The activities are the actions your resources complete or are used for. This should also include the program team as well as your broader organisation. It also describes the target group for your program and includes relevant information such as personas, profiles and journey maps about them.

ASSUMPTIONS

We think of assumptions as risks in disguise. Capturing assumptions is therefore a critically important part of your program logic. Assumptions are the beliefs we have about our program, the people involved, and how it will work. It is worth running a separate risk workshop to capture and assess the likelihood and impact of all the assumptions (risks) on your program and the best approach to treating them.

EXTERNAL FACTORS

When considering external factors we like to group them into PESTLEC, which as we know is political, economic, social, technological, legal, environmental and commercial impacts on your program's outcome or goal.

PROGRAM ROADMAP

Our experience is that these parts should contain on-going elements or programs, and activities that are new or creating new products and services. On-going elements or programs are those activities that are more routine and therefore predictable, but still need to have an outcomes-based focus. Activities that are new or creating new products and services need a greater level of control due to the increased level of risk of achievement.

We recommend tranches, which focus on achievements from an outcome based on the projects' and activities' outputs. Again, these tranches need to be sufficiently close in time to ensure the program achieves outcomes.

At these decision points it is important for the business owner and sponsor to evaluate not only what has been delivered and if it meets the stated expectations, but also what is planned to be delivered in the next stage or tranche.

A decision to progress at these boundaries or gate is made by the sponsor, only if satisfied with both what has been delivered and what is planned to be delivered. Too often we see organisations with these gates defined within the method, but they are wide open, so the programs and projects sail through without a formal go/no-go decision being made.

PROGRAM LOGIC AND EVALUATION

Once your program logic is completed, it is a useful tool for planning your evaluation. The outcomes columns in the project will give you an idea of what you should be trying to measure. It is good to try to measure both short and medium-term outcomes.

It is more difficult to measure the long-term or impact outcomes due to the time it takes for the impact to be realised. There are many external factors that affect it, making it difficult to establish how much of the long-term or impact outcome was the result of your program, and how much was the result of external factors.

To reduce this risk, we recommend that all benefits or final outcomes undertake a DOAM test, which stands for define, observe, attribute and measure. Each benefit should be defined, for example, the Australian government owns the policy to be a carbon neutral economy by 2050, which contributes to a global agreement that Earth's temperature should not increase by more than 2°C. When we reach 2050 this overall goal can be observed and measured by checking the temperature, and the Australian policy goal by assessing our carbon footprint. The four pillars pathway activities and programs should be able to be attributed to this success.

There will likely be activities that were planned to support this goal, but did not. Setting out clear benefits means these activities can be stopped early, or in the case of pet projects, not started. There will also be activities that detract from this goal, but are unlikely to be stopped any time soon, such as using coal-fired power stations, animal agriculture, or travel by planes.

Having a link between the business case and those activities that can attribute to its success is critical, especially when the period of time is large such as with the Australian carbon-neutral 2050 goal. Here we recommend you create a traceability matrix, to enable the drawing of a direct line between work or activities, and benefits. One of our preferred methods to achieve this is using a benefits dependency network (BDN), which maps the value chain from activities through output and outcomes to benefits.

Mapping out interim and final benefits also helps define ownership, which is also a must. If you have owners for each point or node on your BDN, then you enable those with accountability to focus on the right things and manage the risks to them.

Chapter XII

PRIORITISING INITIATIVES

For many organisations the idea of creating a formulaic set of initiatives is not possible. The organisation may be facing significant external forces and the industry in which they operate may be rapidly changing or going through a process of disruption.

In some organisations, the annual budget process produces an allocation of funds for IT projects, investments, asset upgrades or new products, however the budget does not identify the specific initiatives to be undertaken. Many organisations need an approach to determine where their funds should be invested and a system to help prioritise and balance their ever-changing needs.

Adaptive strategy requires a system of regular and adaptive identification and approval of a portfolio of initiatives that are regularly added to, changed and prioritised based on the emerging needs of the organisation. Some of the best innovations and ideas come from customers or from staff in the organisation. This portfolio process allows such ideas and innovations to be captured, prioritised, funded and implemented.

An adaptive strategy can be implemented in a number of simple steps. We will examine each of these steps in turn.

SETTING UP YOUR ADAPTIVE STRATEGY IMPLEMENTATION SYSTEM

Step 1: Identification of initiatives

At any given time there are dozens if not hundreds of initiatives under way in your organisation. Many of them claim to be aligned to the organisation's strategy, however if you examine the actual occurrence, then you will find there is a passing reference at best.

You have probably read in many books or articles that all initiatives should be aligned to the organisation's strategy, strategy plan or goals.

Being "aligned" infers the organisation's strategy will somehow be achieved. Poor alignment creates a major problem — each of the misaligned initiatives spends money, takes up people's time and also sucks up management's intellectual energy.

However, there are two fundamental flaws in the concept of alignment. First, without any measure of alignment there is really no clear way to determine if a project is actually aligned, or whether the proponent of the project is just saying they think it is. Second, without a measure of alignment, there is no way to determine how the strategy will actually be delivered.

A much greater focus is needed, with only initiatives that truly contribute to the strategy being funded and resourced.

For each initiative currently under way, or any that are being planned for the current or short-term future (next six months), the proponent should prepare a two or three-page project proposal. The proposal should articulate:

- background
- deliverables
- rationale
- contribution to achievement of your organisation's strategy
- indicative budget estimate
- key timings
- top three risks
- people and skills required to deliver.

The proposal should be succinct, no more than three pages, and to the point. It should be prepared by the project proponent, often a middle manager, and reviewed and endorsed by their line management.

This proposal process achieves a few benefits. First, it requires the proponent to clearly articulate project deliverables, and contribution to achieving your organisation's strategy. Having reviewed thousands of these proposals over many years, it never ceases to amaze me how many people can't identify why the project is being done or what it will deliver.

Research on strategy implementation failure shows that many of the strategic initiatives are either not good ideas in the first place or are not capable of being implemented. In either case, they should not have funds or people allocated to them.

This proposal process acts as a screening exercise and helps senior management determine the value to the organisation.

Step 2: Prioritisation

To get started, a framework for prioritisation is needed. Many organisations prioritise purely on the RoI, however, this is not necessarily the best or only priority. We have worked with many private and public-sector organisations to create such a framework. The common prioritisation criteria used in government are:

- contribution to policy
- contribution of organisational strategy
- risk reduction
- cost savings.

For the private sector, the prioritisation criteria are most commonly:

- contribution of organisational strategy
- RoI
- risk reduction
- cost savings.

A level of contribution scaling system is needed for each initiative. Typically we have used very simple measures:

- complete contribution
- partial contribution
- enabler
- no identified contribution.

Once this system has been developed, each of the project proposals identified in Step 1 can be analysed to determine the level of contribution against each of the four prioritisation criterion.

Step 3: Analysis

The next step involves the analysis of the proposed initiatives. Most organisations have significantly more initiatives than available funds, therefore it is critically important to determine the combination of initiatives that will provide the optimum result, be that RoI or a contribution to strategy. Many organisations fall down because they look only at the initiatives that meet the above criteria, and do not examine either the readiness of the organisation to make such changes or the capability or capacity to successfully implement.

When implementing projects the rubber hits the road with the supply and availability of specific people with specific skills, expertise and experience. Without this, no project or initiative will get delivered.

An analysis of the skills for each of the prioritised initiatives needs to be undertaken and an assessment made as to the availability of the required resources and a judgment made as to the organisation's ability to deliver.

More sophisticated organisations conduct further analysis to assist in the selection decision making in Step 4, by:

- categorising their initiatives by strategic theme
- examining the proposed initiatives by their level of risk versus their return
- determining the risk versus whether the initiatives deliver a short, medium or long-term benefit.

Graphical methods such as bubble charts are often used to represent each of these analyses.

Step 4: Selection

Following the analysis, the next step is to select the initiatives that will be undertaken over the coming period. Projects that are selected need to be funded and resourced, so it is important that only those that can be fully supported are approved. Research has shown that many organisations don't do this, but instead provide a little bit of funding and resourcing for a much larger group of projects, which results in significant delays and often results in outright failure. Partial investment isn't a viable solution as the projects become starved of the critical resource, or necessary funds or skills when it is most needed, which leads to a series of unrecoverable delays.

Step 5: Balancing and re-prioritising

Many organisations undertake a regular, repeatable process to seek proposals and to analyse, prioritise and approve new initiatives. The most successful and sustainable organisations do this on at least a quarterly basis. Governments often operate one cycle per financial year, coinciding with their annual budget cycle. We have often seen private and public-sector organisations operate two cycles per year, with a major cycle being aligned to the budget process, and the second, smaller cycle, occurring mid-year.

When each proposal approval cycle is undertaken, there are proposals for new initiatives to be considered. There are also existing projects and initiatives that may be under way, and at various points in their delivery lifecycle. During each proposal approval cycle both new and existing projects should be reviewed. Ideally, all existing projects will be progressing as planned and as expected. However, some projects may be not delivering — the proposal review cycle is a good opportunity to reassess the project to determine if it should be put on hold or shut down altogether. In some instances, the project may turn out to be no longer relevant or not as high a priority as a new project that needs funding and resourcing.

This balancing of re-prioritisation process provides the vehicle to adapt and evolve your organisation's strategy and be much more flexible and agile in your implementation efforts.

Chapter XIII

BUSINESS CASE APPROVED, WORK BEGINS

Why a business case?

Every initiative, project, program or strategic initiative requires a reason to justify the investment of money, time or effort. For many organisations, this is not a natural activity, and for others, the business case may be nothing more than a feeble attempt to collect some information that gives some sort of plausible reason to proceed.

We see many invalid business cases where the outcomes or benefits the program or project is expecting to achieve, are not achievable, highly unlikely, or even impossible. Stephen Jenner, one of the world's leading subject matter experts in benefits realisation management, suggests that many executives engage in "benefits fraud"[28]. Very few business cases actually show a real RoI or a valid justification to expend funds.

We often see an over-emphasis of financial control and return, which must be balanced with other drivers. Our belief is we have moved through significant efficiency driven programs and now must focus on effectiveness. Danish academic Bent Flyvbjerg has conducted extensive research on business cases for major projects. His research has shown that the cost estimates used to decide whether such projects should be undertaken are highly and systematically misleading and grossly underestimated. He suggests we should not trust cost estimates and cost-benefit analyses produced by project promoters and their analysts.

Business cases should not just be a one-off event that are produced before an initiative is kicked off. Instead, they should be a yardstick against which to measure the initiative's continued justification and outcomes. Assumptions made during the planning process sometimes turn out to be false, or flawed. The solutions proposed and benefits that will be derived from these solutions have to be validated and change over time.

Developing a business case in phases

Business cases should be the follow-on deliverable from the proposal discussed in Chapter XII. Industry-best practice suggests the business case should occur in three phases.

The strategic outline case holds the high-level aims, goals, case for change, delivery options, cost-benefit analysis components, basis-for-post program evaluation and sufficient information to commence identifying or starting the program.

The outline business case then expands on the strategic outline case to optimise the value the program will deliver, taking into account costs, benefits and risks. It also confirms the approach to delivery, affordability and identifies resources and governance arrangements.

The detailed business case then confirms that value, and that the most economic approach is being taken. It sets out commercial and contractual arrangements and re-confirms affordability and plans for successful delivery of the program.

The detailed business case is then built, articulating fully costed solution options and justification for the recommended option.

The five-case model

Industry-best practices suggests that a detailed business case should address five specific cases: strategic, economic, commercial, financial and management.

Complex project proposals can be developed in three iterations as they discover more about the project through research and analysis.

- The Strategic Outline Case — makes the case for change and a short list of options
- The Outline Business Case — defines the solution that will deliver optimal value for money

- The Full Business Case — takes the solution through procurement, establishing delivery plans and detailed costings

Less complex project proposals can combine all iterations with the depth of evidence proportionate to the risk and value of the proposed investment with transparent trade-offs and visibility to your thinking.

Please note, you still need effective project and program management to deliver the project and manage the risks once you have the funds.

Each of these five cases should be addressed in the strategic outline (proposal), the outline business case, and detailed business case. The level of information within each build increases as you progress through the three business-case development phases.

The 5 Case Model

The 5 key elements of good practice business cases

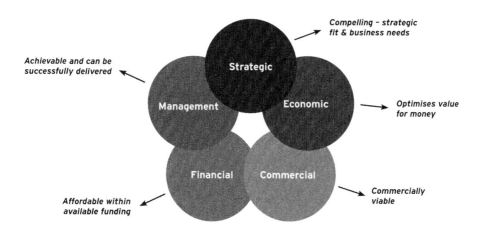

When training people in this method the facilitator draws on *The Elephant's Child* by Rudyard Kipling, where he states the six key items needed for a valid business case — "I keep six honest serving men: (They taught me all I know) their names are What and Where and When and How and Why and Who."

What to look for in a business case?

We have worked with dozens of executives who are presented with business cases to approve. Often the chief financial officer (CFO) is asked to review and provide an analysis of the RoI or determine the net present value or payback period. But a purely financial analysis doesn't always provide the answers needed. In a not-for-profit or a government organisation, RoI may also not be overly relevant, particularly where the initiative is mandated by the minister, or is associated with delivering a program of social benefits or improvement for members.

To help you identify the critical aspects of a business case we have put together a ready reckoner.

There are five questions that you need to gain answers to:

- The strategic case: is there a compelling reason for the change?
- The economic case: does the preferred investment option optimise value for money?
- The commercial case: is the proposed project commercially viable?
- The financial case: is the spending proposal affordable?
- The management case: how can the proposal be delivered successfully?

---

[28] projectagency.co.uk/documents/jenner-benefitsmgt.ppt

Chapter XIV

IMPLEMENTATION MINDSET AND CULTURE

Ensuring successful implementation requires flexibility and adaptability, rather than focusing on the hierarchical command-and-control approach. The agile mindset must lead.

When we think about empowerment, we are really talking about leadership. Empowering your teams to deliver what is needed in an effective manner is a critical leadership trait. We see many executives failing to do this. They interact with their team like seagulls, swooping in from time to time, pecking around for issues and then asking an already stressed team to undertake additional work to satisfy their needs. They leave with no understanding of the chaos they are causing.

Leadership needs to inspire your team into action. Great leaders are those we want to follow rather than have to follow. The management by exception approach is good to leverage because it requires the team to understand the vision and purpose of what they are doing. They need to be motivated to undertake the tasks, and they need to understand where the boundaries are, so when they are forecasting they are going to go over a boundary, they are able to alert their leader and have an approach to gaining support in resolving the issues they are facing.

Two key items that must be in place to achieve this approach are: a forecast at the beginning that they will need help, rather than at a point that is too late, resulting in you forcing your hand; and your approach to their request for help. If a request for help is treated as an issue by you, and the team feel they are not supported in raising these challenges in advance of them occurring, then they are likely to try to resolve the problems themselves. It usually means the challenges they can't solve on their own are much bigger when they reach you. This is probably a key driver of the large quantity of failed projects we have seen for the past 20 years.

This empowerment model does not mean that once the team have funding they go full steam until they run out of money, or hit an issue as described above. The funding and approvals should be broken down into key decision points. At a project level, to maintain sufficient control, we would recommend stages that are aligned to key decision or a planning horizon — a level at which the project team can determine who is working on what, and when it is happening. It could be at an hourly, daily, weekly or monthly level.

For the empowerment model to function effectively it is critical the program or project establish an operating rhythm. This is a rhythm where reporting is undertaken on a regular frequency so the team are aware of the steps needed to get a decision made and/or hear back from a change request.

For programs, we have learnt that when setting up governance frameworks, it is best to establish an operating rhythm on the most significant project, and then build the rhythm of the other projects and initiatives around it. Treating the significant project as a reference around which other projects need to orbit and interact, creates a stable information flow and reduces your concern as reports and meetings are predictable. These meetings are also about to be added to your diary well in advance, assisting better time management.

Talking of concern, we typically get concerned when we do not hear any news. It is also important for the information flows to be transparent. To achieve this, we recommend setting up a collaboration tool, so all program and project stakeholders are able to view the status of the program or project in which they have an interest, and can see when reports are to be generated. Some added advantages of this visibility are; your team reduces the level of ad-hoc reporting and where there is a high volume of ad-hoc reports requested, they can be added to the standard operating rhythm. This further improves the confidence of stakeholders in the project or program.

Action and outcome orientation is critical. Peter Drucker is considered the father of management thinking and one of his famous quotes is:

"Culture eats strategy for breakfast." His excellent article on Thought Management[29] follows this with "... if culture is for breakfast then structure is for lunch".

The point here is your teams will not fit neatly into organisational chart boxes and as you know, these charts, once created, are normally out of date anyway.

A cultural element we have seen with open information is, where people do have access to information they feel more a part of your organisation, more trusted and therefore more motivated to help achieve your organisational goals.

With all this success, questions are being asked about their societal roles. Are they givers or takers. Adam M. Grant is an American psychologist and author who is currently a professor at the Wharton School of the University of Pennsylvania specialising in organisational psychology. His book *Give And Take* describes this succinctly. It appears Uber has fallen hardest on this issue, with its CEO Travis Kalanick resigning over toxic culture. Questions are being asked of Facebook with Mark Zuckerberg now employing an army of people to fix harassment and interference issues and the change from a people-oriented decentralised model. Facebook's "give people the power" has moved to a centralised tech company-driven model, where many people see a "big brother" taking all the power.

In Australia we have also experienced similar issues, especially in the banking and finance sector, with a royal commission addressing ongoing misconduct. These issues have been created by a culture of takers, and as "everyone is doing it", many within this sector have accepted these behaviours as normal practice.

These challenges can be addressed by taking a longer-term win, win, win approach, which may not achieve the same levels of financial achievement in the short term, but is more likely to last due to the right culture, exhibited by visible rituals, and habits.

We think technology can help with transparency, where people can see the purpose and the tasks being done to achieve that purpose and therefore assess the value associated with these tasks, so they can then support each other to mutual success.

To achieve this goal of transparency it will be important for you to take a holistic approach to your technology. Include not only your staff, but the work your contractors, consultants and partners are undertaking for you. This approach will ensure you are able to adapt more quickly when you need to and be able to better manage the value — not just at the start, but ongoing value of what is being worked on and delivered by each party.

Another key element of an implementation culture is skilled staff. Again, too often we see staff, contractors and consultants performing tasks in which they are not trained, skilled or experienced. We find this is usually due to organisational pressures to use internal staff to reduce additional costs, and with contractors and consultants there is usually an emotive element because they know and like the person or brand.

To have an implementation culture it is critical to ensure that your team have the right mix of skills and experience, otherwise you may save money short term but the delivery team are unlikely to be efficient or effective, costing you more long term and potentially implementation failure as avoidable problems (risks) occur.

GOVERNING STRATEGIC INITIATIVES

Effective strategy implementation requires the application of approropriate governance to ensure decisions are being made by the right people at the right time, and to deal with any issues that arise.

From the thousands of reviews we have completed over the past 10 years, we see effective program and project governance only achieved where the chief executive values the discipline of project management and invests in having a PMO support programs, and the projects establish the right level of governance to set themselves up for success.

We have come to the conclusion that there is a significant improvement needed in the way initiatives are governed. Executives must be held to account to achieve the outcomes aligned to organisational or government goals, and sponsors should be held to account to deliver the programs and projects against these outcomes.

What is governance?

Governance is the framework by which an organisation is directed and controlled. Good governance is about the processes for making and implementing decisions. It's not about making "correct" decisions, but about the best possible process for making those decisions.

Good decision-making processes, and therefore good governance, share several characteristics. All have a positive effect on various aspects of local government including consultation policies and practices, meeting procedures, service quality protocols, councillor and officer conduct, role clarification and good working relationships.

Effective governance structures encourage organisations to create value, through entrepreneurialism, innovation, development and exploration, and provide accountability and control systems commensurate with the risks involved.

There is no single model of good governance.

Governance frameworks

Governance frameworks have been developed to communicate the relationship between different levels of governance in an organisation. This is of particular importance in the context of strategy implementation and project delivery where a delineation of responsibility between the company board, project sponsors, and project managers is required.

The term "governance of project management" clearly identifies the different applications of governance, and shows the interface of corporate governance and project management. These elements will be discussed later.

When we examine corporate governance in the context of projects, programs and other change initiatives, it is important to understand the key activities and functions that are undertaken.

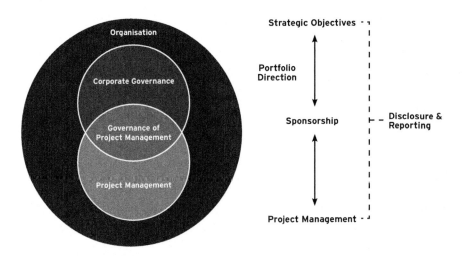

Governance framework for projects

Strategic objectives are established by the board of the organisation and are communicated through their strategic plan. These objectives and goals are used in identifying, selecting and prioritising projects and programs as part of the organisation's portfolio management approach.

A governance body such as the strategic investment committee or IT investment board sets portfolio direction and involves establishing the desired portfolio mix and determining appropriate selection criteria and weightings to ensure a balance is achieved.

Sponsorship is a function that exists at the project and program level; a role that may be performed by an individual or a group, such as a project steering committee or a program board. For large or more mature organisations, a specific governance framework may exist to provide oversight for the hundreds or even thousands of projects operating at any given time.

Project management is the function of managing the delivery of the specific project. It is important to understand that project management is not a governance function per se, however the project manager undertakes a governance function, and the project manager must operate within the context of project governance.

Disclosure and reporting is a key principle of governance, and is a practice embedded in project management, governance of project management and corporate governance. Development of reports not only aids in communication and information dissemination, but reports also capture the status at a given point in time and form part of the corporate record.

The governance framework will be unique for each organisation however it will conform to the following range of key principles.

- Promote transparent and fair markets, and the efficient allocation of resources. It should be consistent with the rule of law and support effective supervision and enforcement.
- Protect and facilitate the exercise of shareholders' rights and ensure the equitable treatment of all shareholders, including minority and foreign shareholders. All shareholders should have the opportunity to obtain effective redress for violation of their rights.
- Provide sound incentives throughout the investment chain and provide for stock markets to function in a way that contributes to good corporate governance.
- Recognise the rights of stakeholders established by law or through mutual agreements and encourage active co-operation between them and corporations to create wealth, jobs, and the sustainability of financially sound enterprises.
- Ensure that timely and accurate disclosure is made on all material matters regarding the corporation, including the financial situation, performance, ownership, and governance of the company.
- Ensure the strategic guidance of the company, the effective monitoring of management by the board, and the board's accountability to the company and the shareholders.

CORPORATE GOVERNANCE

Corporate governance involves a set of relationships between a company's management, its board, its shareholders and other stakeholders. Corporate governance also provides the structure through which the objectives of the company are set, and the means of attaining those objectives and monitoring performance are determined.

Corporate governance occurs at a whole-of-organisation level with a major focus on BAU operations. Good corporate governance should provide proper incentives for the board and management to pursue objectives that are in the interests of the company and its shareholders and should facilitate effective monitoring.

Many stock exchanges around the world have specified and published particular requirements for listed companies. In the United Kingdom, for example, the Corporate Governance Code sets standards of good practice in relation to board leadership and effectiveness, remuneration, accountability and relations with shareholders. Taking a principle-based approach the code sets forth rules for operation of publicly listed companies.

These principles are intended to help policy makers evaluate and improve the legal, regulatory, and institutional framework for corporate governance, with a view to support economic efficiency, sustainable growth and financial stability. This is primarily achieved by providing shareholders, board members and executives as well as financial intermediaries and service providers with the right incentives to perform their roles within a framework of checks and balances.

The principles recognise the interests of employees and other stakeholders and their important role in contributing to the long-term success and performance of the company. Other factors relevant to a company's decision-making processes, such as environmental, anti-corruption or ethical concerns, are considered in the principles but are treated more explicitly in a number of other instruments including the Organisation for Economic Co-operation and Development (OECD) Guidelines for Multinational Enterprises, the Convention on Combating Bribery of Foreign Public Officials in International Business Transactions, the United Nations (UN) Guiding Principles on Business and Human Rights, and the International Labour Organization (ILO) Declaration on Fundamental Principles and Rights at Work, which are referenced in the Principles.

GOVERNANCE OF PROJECT MANAGEMENT

Governance, as it applies to strategy implementation, requires the application of specific practices to the portfolio of strategic initiatives and comprises the value system, responsibilities, processes and policies that allow projects to achieve organisational activities and foster implementation that is in the best interests of all stakeholders, both internal and external, and the corporation itself.

Governance of project management is the responsibility of corporate management requiring the support of project sponsors, project managers and project teams. Effective governance of project management will ensure the organisation's projects are aligned to its strategic objectives, delivered efficiently, and are sustainable.

The relationships between management responsibilities are shown in the diagram below. This shows the activities involved in the governance of project management is a subset of corporate governance. It shows that most project management activities are outside the responsibility of corporate governance. This suggests that the control of projects must be shared between corporate governance and project management.

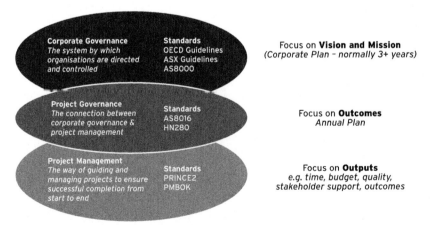

Governance hierarchy

PROJECT GOVERNANCE

Project governance is a set of management systems, rules, protocols, relationships and structures that provide the framework within which decisions are made for project development and implementation to achieve the intended business or strategic motivation (Bekker & Steyn).

Project governance is specific to the delivery of projects and change within an organisation. It is an oversight function that occurs throughout the project lifecycle and typically includes:

- acceptance criteria for success and deliverables
- an escalation process
- organisational charts and defined roles and responsibilities
- lifecycle and methodology
- stage gate or phase reviews.

Project governance may include subjects such as defining the management structure; the policies, processes and methodologies to be used; limits of authority for decision making; stakeholder responsibilities and accountabilities; and interactions such as reporting and the escalation of issues or risks.

The responsibility for maintaining the appropriate governance of a project is usually assigned either to the project sponsor or to a project steering committee (ISO 21500 Section 3.6).

Project governance:
- provides a framework for ethical decision making
- is based on transparency, accountability and defined roles
- sets parameters for management action
- defines project goals and the means by which they should be achieved.

PORTFOLIO GOVERNANCE

Portfolio governance focuses on the roles and responsibilities for portfolio management and ensuring appropriate decision-making process and organisational controls are in place and functioning effectively and efficiently. It includes establishment and maintenance of structures, procedures and methods in order to maintain correct governance of projects and programs within the portfolio.

Portfolio governance decisions include:

- acceptance of projects into the portfolio based upon the organisation's strategy, the portfolio optimisation strategy and the organisation's capabilities
- prioritising projects, including start, end suspension and termination
- allocation of resources to projects based on project priorities
- identification of skills bottlenecks, which risk delays in delivery of projects within the portfolio
- possible remedies and mitigation strategies for any risks or issues encountered within the portfolio.

PROGRAM GOVERNANCE

Thiry suggests that program governance consists of developing the vision and objective, business strategy and stakeholder needs. Effective program governance involves putting in place the right structures and allocating the resources necessary to achieve the vision. Finally, it means putting in place the necessary monitoring and control systems to make the right decisions and realign the program if necessary.

The focus of program governance is efficiency. It should develop a fit-for-purpose product that can accommodate constant adaptation of project outcomes to changing market needs. In doing so, program governance requires:

- developing a program vision and objectives
- putting in place the right structures for decision making
- allocating resources to achieve the vision
- putting in place necessary monitoring and control systems
- overseeing benefits management
- ensuring project business cases are sound and in line with the program vision.

CHARACTERISTICS OF GOOD GOVERNANCE

Participation

All involved should have a voice in decision making, either directly or through legitimate intermediate institutions that represent their interests. Such broad participation is built on freedom of association and speech, as well as capacity to participate constructively.

Rule of law

Legal frameworks should be fair and enforced impartially, particularly the laws on human rights.

Transparency

Transparency is built on the free flow of information. Processes, institutions and information are directly accessible to those concerned with them, and enough information is provided to understand and monitor them.

Responsiveness

Institutions and processes try to serve all stakeholders.

Consensus orientation

Good governance mediates differing interests to reach a broad consensus on what is in the best interests of the group and, where possible, on policies and procedures.

Equity

All men and women have opportunities to improve or maintain their well-being.

Effectiveness and efficiency

Processes and institutions produce results that meet needs while making the best use of resources.

Accountability

Decision makers in government, the private sector and civil society organisations are accountable to the public, as well as to institutional stakeholders. This accountability differs depending on the organisations and whether the decision is internal or external to an organisation.

Strategic vision

Leaders and the public have a broad and long-term perspective on good governance and human development, along with a sense of what is needed for such development. There is also an understanding of the historical, cultural and social complexities in which that perspective is grounded.

Enhance prospects for success

True project success is gauged by the realisation of business benefits, not only the on-time, on-budget delivery of outputs. Potential for success and value to the business increases when senior business managers actively participate in project governance throughout the project lifecycle. This includes decision making and promoting the organisational change needed to achieve the anticipated business value. Failure factors such as inadequate information, unclear requirements, inadequate resourcing and poor communication are more likely to be identified and addressed earlier when good governance arrangements are in place.

Senior management responsibility

Directors and senior managers are ultimately responsible for the success of organisational projects and business strategy. While responsibility for some aspects of projects may be delegated to others, senior managers remain accountable for effective, efficient and acceptable use of organisational resources including IT investments. Ensuring adequate oversight of significant projects is important for being informed and maintaining accountability.

Sound investment decisions

Good project governance helps an organisation ensure its investments contribute positively to overall organisational performance, especially through:

- giving priority to projects that have the greatest value to the organisation and align with business objectives
- requiring that projects deliver all elements of change necessary to achieve desired outcomes, especially with regard to people, process, structure and technology.

THE IMPACT OF POOR GOVERNANCE

According to Caravel (2013) "A Review of Project Governance Effectiveness in Australia", on average 48% of projects fail to meet their baseline time, cost and quality objectives. While the project team is more often than not blamed, it is believed the actual cause of failure comes down to a lack of governance. The following table from Caravel's review illustrates the impact of governance basics on the success of projects.

SUCCESS CRITERIA	YES	NO
Approved governance plans exist	13%	87%
Governance team member position descriptions have project governance KPIs	17%	83%
Governance team member performance is measured	6%	94%
Governance team performance is measured	9%	91%
Project governance skills adequate	20%	80%
Governance team members have no conflicts of interest	30%	70%
Governance team and project team have adequate financial authority	45%	55%
Governance team members exhibit proper corporate behaviour	45%	55%
Governance team understand difference between business consultants, solution subject matter experts (SME) and project delivery SMEs	30%	70%

Governance success criteria

The following graph from Caravel's 2013 report reinforces the range of issues that are commonplace and that reduce the effectiveness of governance systems.

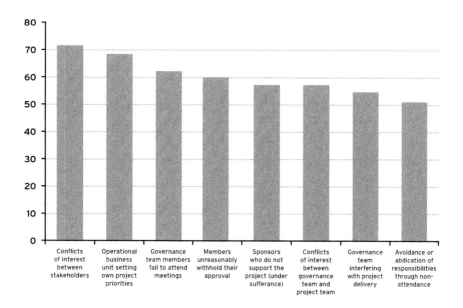

Governance Issues

ESTABLISHING GOVERNANCE ARRANGEMENTS

So, how does a project manager develop or improve a governance system for the project and what factors need to be considered? Processes, procedure, people and tools are the ways in which a governance framework is delivered throughout the project lifecycle. Project complexity is a factor in designing appropriate governance, although often cost is a driver too. As explained earlier, one of the challenges as project manager is finding and maintaining the right balance between managing risk and maintaining operational efficiency.

Developing the governance plan

Developing, documenting and communicating a governance plan ensures a shared understanding of the governance standards, roles and responsibilities relevant to the project. Arrangements are sometimes documented within the project plan, or can be the subject of a separate governance plan, but should include:

- clear statements of roles, responsibilities and performance criteria for the governance of project management, including any delegated authorities for project decisions
- authorisation points at which the business case is reviewed and approved
- specific criteria for reporting project status and for the escalation of risks and issues to the levels required by the organisation
- identifying who is responsible for deciding when independent scrutiny of projects and project management systems is required, and who implements such scrutiny.

There may also be requirements for the engagement of project stakeholders, to ensure they are involved at a level commensurate with their importance to the organisation and in a manner that fosters trust. Governance arrangements also frequently seek to ensure the organisation fosters a culture of improvement and of frank internal disclosure of project information.

Delegated authorities can be added to role and position descriptions to reinforce accountability and performance expectations.

These sorts of broad overall requirements are key to the successful governance of all projects within the organisation, and it is the project manager's responsibility to ensure they are familiar with, and comply with, the appropriate project governance requirements.

Projects steering committee

As an example of typical governance arrangements, a project steering committee within an organisation might be responsible for:

- identifying business priorities based on business plans
- ensuring projects meet identified business strategies
- ensuring identified business benefits are delivered
- delegation of agreed funding
- monitoring key project milestone achievements
- reviewing risk control and issue control reports
- assisting with the resolution of project issues.

Governance policies and procedures

Projects also need to be undertaken in ways that align with organisational governance requirements. Mature organisations will have defined governance mechanisms that clarify the responsibilities of different individuals and groups for different aspects of the project. Note however, that existing functional authorities in an organisation may not align perfectly to the needs of a project.

Existing governance arrangements might include:

- overall responsibility for project management — this may lie with the board of directors for a private enterprise organisation, or with a departmental secretary (or similar) for a government agency
- project/s steering committee, which may have oversight of all projects, a group of projects or an individual project
- purchasing/preferred supplier arrangements
- in government agencies, the FMA Act and agency-specific procurement documentation
- communications frameworks and authority to speak on behalf of the project
- financial delegations.

Any existing delegated authorisation bodies need to have sufficient representation, competence, authority and resources to enable them to make appropriate decisions.

We have worked with many organisations helping them establish their governance arrangements. As we approach this task, we work with executives such as yourself, to push decision making as far down into the organisation as possible with the aim of freeing up executives to focus on their leadership activities, and empowering their teams to deliver the outcomes and achieve the goals defined by the leaders.

---

[29] https://thoughtmanagement.org/2013/07/10/culture-eats-your-structure-for-lunch/

Chapter XV

SPONSORING STRATEGIC INITIATIVES

Any change or strategic initiative delivered in your organisation is an investment. It may not be necessarily a large investment, or purely an investment of actual funds, but it is always an investment that chews up people's time and takes up a certain amount of intellectual space in managers' minds. Like a financial investment, any strategic initiative requires executive oversight.

Every strategic initiative needs an executive sponsor: someone who can provide guidance and direction to the implementation team; someone who can make decisions when needed and someone who can help the manager or leader of the initiative resolve any issues or overcome any roadblocks or obstacles. The sponsor isn't the project manager nor are they involved in the day-to-day details, but instead sit at arm's length, and in doing so can often provide a perspective that those involved are too close to really see or appreciate.

We mentioned before the need to consider outcomes and benefits, and a leader needing to inspire their team into action. It is also important the team know the role they must play in taking the necessary action. One key element in the team's defined roles and responsibilities is the need to align roles of the sponsor and business owners to achievement of outcomes, as well as ensure their roles and responsibilities are regularly evaluated and re-aligned to outcomes where changes are needed. It is our experience that all too often executive roles and responsibilities, which drive their behaviour and performance, are not aligned to the best long-term interests of the organisation and are therefore value detractors rather than value creators.

We have learnt that having an executive sponsor for each program is essential. This is the executive who has the most to lose should the program not succeed, but does not have time to be actively involved in the program, which is a key requirement of the person fulfilling the role of program sponsor.

SO WHAT DOES THE SPONSOR DO?

The sponsor plays a critical role in the governance of individual projects and/or programs. Best practice identifies a number of key actions and responsibilities that all sponsors should take on. We will examine each of these in turn:

1. Own and approve the project business case

The sponsor owns and approves the business case for the project. The sponsor is the single executive in the organisation responsible and accountable for the outcome of the strategic initiative. Their role is to ensure the strategic initiative or project delivers the benefits outlined in the business case. Given this role, it is therefore imperative that the sponsor ensures the business case is realistic and achievable and able to be delivered.

2. Engage with peers in the organisation to manage relationships and politics

Strategic initiatives and projects are not done by individuals but instead are delivered by teams of people working together focused on a common goal or objective. Like all activities that involve many people, communication, engagement and relationship building is absolutely critical. In the absence of these actions, there are misunderstandings, conflicts can occur and confusion can exist between people as to what the aims of the strategic initiative are or what it will deliver.

A key role of the sponsor is to engage with peers across the organisation and to communicate, and if needed, advocate for the project. On occasions, this may require managing the "politics" to ensure the project team can get on and deliver, and not get distracted by the personalities and games that exist in some organisations.

3. Serve as a focus point for decisions beyond the project manager's scope of authority

Project managers are largely focused on the project, and rightly so. One of the downsides of this high level of focus is the project manager's tendency to be blind to external factors happening outside the project. We also find that the project manager often has limited authority in the organisation and in most cases does not have a financial delegation to approve expenditure or have authority to hire (or fire) employees or contractors.

The sponsor plays a crucial role as decision maker where the decisions are beyond the project manager's authority. Any good project manager should come to you as a sponsor with a number of options and their recommendations, rather than coming to you with a problem and wanting you to come up with a solution.

4. Act swiftly and decisively to resolve conflicts

Sponsors often need to step in and facilitate the resolution of any conflicts that may exist, be they between the project team and other parts of the organisation, or with an external supplier or stakeholder. Conflicts often arise due to simple communications breakdowns or misunderstandings between people who are being asked to change what they do, often in a stressful and uncertain environment.

Conflicts are an inevitable result of such an environment. As a sponsor, being at arms length from the day-to-day, you often have a level of clarity that comes with this distance, and as such, you can often view conflict situations with a fresh set of eyes and identify a potential way forward. Those involved in the project may have a vested interest or believe in a specific solution being needed and can be clouded by their closeness to the issue at hand.

Unlike good wine or cheese, problems and conflicts do not improve if left unattended. The sponsor needs to intervene and act swiftly and decisively to resolve them.

5. Review the viability of a project against critical success criteria at stage and phase gates

We have identified that projects are often delivered in phases or stages. The business case and the project plan developed at the start of the project is a best-guess and an approximation of what will be done, and when. The plan identifies what will be spent and who will do what. But like all plans and estimates, they start to change and evolve over time. Assumptions made during the planning phase may turn out to be incomplete, flawed or may simply become overtaken by events. External factors may result in the project being no longer relevant or may result in the end product needing to be altered or even delivered more quickly than initially thought. Issues also often arise throughout the implementation, with people coming and going from the organisation, people getting sick or systems failing testing despite everyone's best efforts during the design and build. Estimates may also be inaccurate, meaning activities may take longer than planned.

No plan ever survives first contact with the enemy.
Field Marshal Helmuth Karl Bernhard Graf von Moltke

At the end of each stage the ongoing viability of the project should be assessed to determine whether the project should continue, be put on hold, or cancelled and shutdown. The sponsor plays a key role in reviewing the ongoing viability of the project.

6. Undertake acceptance of project deliverables at handover and project sign off

Given the sponsor is responsible for the outcome of the project and the benefits the project delivers, they should play a key role in ensuring the project has been fully delivered by the project manager and project team. When the project is finalised and the "solution" is handed over to the organisation (often an operational area) for ongoing use, delivery and management, the project team then pack up and walk away, particularly if they are externally contracted resources. If the project has not been fully delivered, if there are any ongoing glitches or technical issues, or there has been insufficient knowledge transfer between the project team and the receiving operations team, this may pose a significant risk to the organisation and may impact on its ability to achieve the desired benefits as outlined in the initial business case.

7. Conduct benefits realisation reviews

As we identified earlier in this chapter, the sponsor is responsible for the business case and achieving the organisation's approved project outcomes. To do so requires identifying the benefits in the business case before the project commences, and monitoring these achievements throughout the lift of the project. Typically, a single project does not deliver many of the project benefits. In most instances, a project puts in place an enabling process, technology, solution or business system, and the business should use these outputs in some way, or in combination with the outputs of other projects, to achieve the anticipated benefits. For example, if the organisation implements a new payroll system that provides particular efficiencies, such benefits cannot be obtained unless business processes surrounding the use of the payroll system are refined and optimised, and the staff previously required to operate a manual system are redeployed.

HOW MANY PROJECTS SHOULD I SPONSOR?

We recommend the sponsor has not more than three programs or programs of work they are sponsoring, so they are able to invest time to proactively get involved rather than be reactive to issues or solely engage in the project when the monthly or quarterly steering committees come around.

The thinking behind three programs is one large and two more operational, an example being a transformation program and two operational programs. That way, along with your operational role, an appropriate level of time can be invested within the programs.

If you split your time into thirds, one-third is focused on the transformation program, one-third your other programs, and one-third your operational duties. Having this approach will help you establish an operating rhythm that will ensure you don't neglect one or more programs because operational matters capture your attention, or vice versa.

As a program sponsor, you should be supported by other executives who are also impacted by the programs you are sponsoring, their formal appointment to the program board or steering committee will greatly improve holistic decision making. The role of these fellow members of your steering committee is to provide you advice and guidance on the program to aid the decisions you need to make and the supporting activities you undertake.

They too should also undertake supporting activities, because they will after all be operating the product or services your program is delivering. We see the greatest program value if they have come from groups or divisions that are positively impacted by the program, and their performance agreements should also align to the program's success measures.

We have learnt that program sponsorship is something that is not just picked up, it is a role that needs to be taught, especially for executives who have little program or project management experience but in-depth knowledge of their area of business. These executives will naturally focus on the technical aspects of your programs and not necessarily the technical elements of program or project management, which are discipline domains in their own right.

We recommend that as a sponsor you train yourself in what is required to be a high-performing sponsor, and seek support from your PMO to help use these additional people and program performance skills to complement your technical skills.

Chapter XVI

STRATEGY IMPLEMENTATION CAPABILITY

Throughout this book we have discussed a number of critical topics that are required for successful strategy implementation. Each of these items has been described in a somewhat isolated manner, however in reality, everything is interconnected and a specific element, such as prioritisation, cannot be isolated out from everything else. Instead, the interconnected system of strategy implementation practices needs to be built within your organisation.

Like human resources, legal, finance, engineering and operations, strategy implementation is a discipline that should exist in your organisation. As with each of these functions, strategy implementation needs a home: a location in the organisation where the SI discipline can grow and be supported. So what is needed to build and support your organisation's strategy implementation capability?

STRATEGY IMPLEMENTATION OFFICE

To gain this consistency across your organisation, a central team should continuously assess the latest trends and incorporate them into your delivery methodology. This emerging multi-method or bi-modal approach also needs ownership and we recommend this is a core responsibility of your strategy implementation office (SIO).

Your SIO is a key support mechanism and provides you with external information that may positively or negatively impact your program. It should support you obtaining resources or people with specialist skills outside of your direct reports. It should also help ensure the risks that may impact other programs are communicated to them.

If you are working for an organisation that has a mature program operating model, then your SIO should also be providing your assurance support, where it aligns external reviews to your biggest risks and helps reduce external reporting. It should also provide you with program practice area support, such as managing benefits and risks.

Your SIO should not only be able to maintain the various methods but help define which method is most appropriate to use for a set of tasks, and support the delivery teams in using the methods. And when it comes to the boundaries of activities and the gates where go/no-go decisions are made, your SIO should make an assessment of the right method and include it in the decision-making process.

The SIO is also able to help maintain cross-functional team or initiative dependencies to ensure there is visibility of progress and a better understanding of needs by the team/s that are receiving the new products or services. This support is especially important when it comes to transitioning to on-going teams using a new product or service.

There are many benefits of having a SIO supporting you define your strategic plan and ensure your organisation is set up to deliver against its objectives.

BUSINESS PROCESSES AND SYSTEMS

Success will arrive if you create and lead a high-performing team. We recommend these teams are grouped into three core disciplines or tribes: a decision-making group supportive of your goals and with a vested interest in their success; a management team able to translate the strategic objectives and goals into new practices and associated products and services; and a "doing" team skilled and experienced in the area they are working on to complete the tasks and activities in the most efficient way.

These three tribes need to feel part of your bigger tribe and that they understand their roles and responsibilities in supporting your higher-level goals. To achieve this within programs[30], we recommend you create a core team, made up of a subset of decision makers and supporters that help the sponsor lead the program to achieve its outcomes and objectives.

Depending on the size and scale of your program, the core team should include your sponsor or program director, your discipline leads or divisional senior representatives who cover the changes your BAU teams must make, your SIO manager, and your SIO co-ordinator. As we say, the SIO is a critical element to your success.

This core team should be at the heart of your program and create a rhythm to which the program operates. The rhythm should include frequency of governance meetings, and workflow of decision making, so it is clear to all stakeholders how decisions are made and that there are sufficient controls and transparency of the decision-making process.

When thinking about the roles of your teams, they should include those responsible for delivery, who must have their work in a plan. This plan could follow agile methods such as inclusion in a Sprint or Kanban chart; a more linear approach captured within a Gantt chart; or other tools that help those managing see where team members are planned to work. The approach you take to controlling the work will depend on the work being done.

A team of contractors, consultants and third-party suppliers or partners are most likely supporting your delivery team. From a management perspective we recommend treating contractors like your employees. They should receive training, but we recommend they do not get paid to attend the training, which is a helpful selling point for those full-time staff who may feel contractors are getting a better deal than them. It is important to train contractors because they need the skills to perform at a high level too, and if they are not using the latest practices then ultimately it is your goals that will be impacted.

Full-time employees should have career pathway plans, and the work they perform should be aligned to achieving these plans. They also receive benefits such as holidays and other leave, which contractors do not receive.

The consultants and partners should have clear performance targets. Where possible they should be weighted to lead indicators so their performance towards the goals are assessed, rather than a backward-looking appraisal of what has been achieved. An example of a performance target may be if you have an IT company supporting your IT system; a performance metric would be the quantity of similar issues raised impacting your business. Password reset is a good example, thanks to all the passwords we have to remember, then forget, and have to reset. This should be an automated or self-service approach. We also see vendors closing cases, but the case should only be closed once the user is satisfied it is closed, rather than the supplier closing to meet a performance target.

Here we have seen partner companies close IT issues once they think they have been resolved, and ask the person with the issue to raise a new issue if it is still a problem. In this case the company was paid per issue closed, but a better metric would have been issue resolved.

We also recommend you ensure that each program has a customer team. These team members are your real, actual customers and they are brought in to be involved in the development of your new practices, products and services. Having your actual customers involved will greatly assist you and your teams in working on the right problems or opportunities.

COMMUNITY OF PRACTICE

The next key structure required to support your strategy implementation capability is a community of practice (CoP)[31].

CoPs are able to share approaches being taken in different areas of your organisation and in fact the CoPs we have established have been most successful when opened up to a wider audience than just your organisation.

You are able to create your own CoP, or most disciplines already have CoPs in which you can join and interact with members for free or at a minimal charge.

Are you a member of a CoP or professional association, or perhaps a CoP within a professional association? If not then we recommend you start exploring and go along to some events to see if they are of value to you. You will find many events listed on Meetup or Eventbrite and other online platforms as well as professional associations listing their events.

---

[30] www.modernprogrammanagement.com
[31] en.wikipedia.org/wiki/Community_of_practice

Chapter XVII

BUILDING YOUR IMPLEMENTATION TEAM

Implementation is a team sport. Implementation requires effort by a multidisciplinary team of people, each of them undertaking a specific series of activities or actions which when grouped together, results in the plan being implemented and the desired outcome achieved.

But this is all great in theory. We know many executives struggle to pull together a team with the right skills, experience and capabilities available at the point when needed. There are many circumstances that make this a somewhat impossible challenge. For starters, the idea of having an ideal team is an elusive somewhat mythical undertaking. Rarely do you have the exact team you need, in the right numbers and with the right levels of skills and the right track record of experience. More often than not, even if you have the right number of people to do the job, the team lacks specific skills, and most individuals have not done something similar before.

On top of this, with the fast pace at which you need to operate, and compounding of changing needs, any plan rapidly becomes out of date.

So what is the answer?

From our experience over many years, we have identified a number of key considerations.

WHAT SKILLS ARE NEEDED?

Implementation requires a specific set of skills. In the same way the CFO and head of legal have a specialist set of skills developed through tertiary study and many years of hands-on experience, so does the project or program manager.

So how do you work out what skills are needed?

The primary role of a project or program manager is to develop a detailed plan to implement an initiative. As part of this planning process, a resource forecast and resource schedule is produced. This schedule will determine "what skills are needed when" and in what volume.

Once the resource forecast has been developed then the project or program manager can advise the sponsor the requirements to deliver the strategic initiative. This may not be a pretty picture, however, as more often than not the detailed plan will show the initiative will require exponentially more people and cost 5-10 times more than was first expected, which is often more money and people than the organisation has available to allocate to any initiative. If this occurs, then some tough decisions need to be made.

A DEDICATED IMPLEMENTATION TEAM

Another common issue we have come across, often due to the limited availability of the number of people and required skills, is that initiatives are given to operational or BAU teams to implement in addition to their day job. This is a recipe for disaster and if done will almost certainly result in not only the strategic initiatives failing, but will also likely result in key members of the team packing up and leaving the organisation.

Successful strategy implementation requires a discrete and dedicated team. This team should report to the executive sponsoring the specific initiative. The implementation team's top priority is delivering the initiative — delivery should not be considered a mere "side hustle". Even when the mathematics of a person's available time add up, there are a number of key limitations that impact someone's ability to deliver.

Research shows there are a number of limiting factors that prevent successful implementation.

First, each person has a certain mental bandwidth and intellectual capacity to deal with multiple competing tasks. While more senior staff have often developed their ability to juggle many things, the mental dexterity to deal with many discrete and often disparate tasks takes energy, and results in a cost of switching. Given the complexity of these initiatives, and the potential impacts they have across the organisation and its medium to long-term future, they take a lot of thinking time.

Second, over time, people develop habits and routines in the way they perform their work. Operationally focused work often involves the completion of repetitive processes, concentrating on efficiency and process compliance. Project-based work, on the other hand, often involves undertaking one-off activities. From our experience, employees performing each of these types of work not only have a different way of operating, but also has a different mindset and perspective towards risk, uncertainty, and ambiguity. Operational workers tend to like a high level of certainty, low risk and limited ambiguity, otherwise they may find they become anxious, stressed or unproductive. Project-based workers on the other hand tend to be turned off by repetition, are more comfortable in dealing with risk and can cope with higher levels of uncertainty and ambiguity. Project-based workers are often problem-solvers who see the project as a challenge to overcome.

When it comes to delivering strategic change, research shows the differences in workers' habits, routines and mindset is critical. A process-based, operational worker will mostly find it difficult to think about what they do in a different way, and are therefore unable to conceive another way of doing things. While they may be able to incrementally improve what they do, a radical change is too far beyond their existing habits and routine. To make more than just incremental changes, a project-based approach is needed, as the implementation requires solving problems, reconceptualising the way in which things are done. This results in moderate to high levels of risk, uncertainty and ambiguity. Most certainly, it is not effective and may not even be possible, to have operational resources implement strategy.

Third, as discussed earlier, large organisations often operate in a hierarchy. This means most teams and executives operate in their own division, which is a silo. Hierarchical organisations tend to limit communication across the organisation and focus up and down the chain of command. With multi-disciplinary and cross-functional teams required to successfully implement strategy and with many strategic initiatives having an impact across multiple divisions, a lack of effective horizontal communication leads to many problems.

Last, many of the performance measurement and bonus schemes used in the modern organisation are siloed as well — KPIs specific to the one division. These incentives often encourage executives to look after their own patch rather than provide any incentive or benefit for working with other executives, helping each other to deliver or to work together to solve cross-functional problems.

These challenges don't just exist within the executives at the top of each division, but rather they occur at all management levels throughout the organisation. It is therefore critical for you to ensure that silos between these teams are managed and that all managers share a common goal and their performance incentives are focused on collaboration and joint outcomes, rather than individual inputs. Our belief is this is where huge amounts of value fall through your organisation, that is, between the gaps of your groups, divisions and business units.

DEALING WITH MULTIPLE MASTERS

Being successful in strategy implementation requires a dual operating model and in doing so you create what has been referred to as an ambidextrous organisation: one that operates a traditional operational or BAU model, and a project-based, change-focused operating model in parallel. Each operating model requires a system of work with associated policies, procedures and supporting administrative and IT systems, however, they are likely to be very different in each operating model.

Many successful organisations operate a matrix structure whereby implementation teams are located in a specific division and draw upon resources from across other divisions as needed for each specific project.

Having a matrix approach does increase complexity to your manager's job, however, if you have put in place the right habits or rituals such as creating a resource pool with visible or transparent resource lists to all your managers, as well as each person's allocation, then managing their tasks is more scientific than political. With a matrix-based structure we are confident you will reduce value loss and are therefore more likely to achieve your strategic goals.

A matrix model is not without its challenges. Individuals have two masters to serve. They report day to day to their team leader or manager, however they also need to report to a project manager, purely for the purposes of the project's initiative. This can create a situation of conflicting priorities whereby the manager identifies one activity as the highest priority, but the project manager identifies some other activity as the highest priority. To be successful, a matrix model requires project managers to accurately estimate and forecast when specific individuals are needed, and the team leader or manager of that section needs to be adept at resource management and servicing the demands of projects.

We have helped many clients developing a heatmap to assess the demand of resources from the projects, then the availability of the BAU staff to support this demand. If you have not undertaken an assessment of this type before, you will see some of your BAU team are significantly over-allocated to projects and therefore the likelihood of that project succeeding is very low, due to a lack of available resources. This often leads to complete failure of any strategic initiative.

Unfortunately, this approach is not a one-time activity as the data on who is doing what will quickly become out of date, so we recommend once you have taken the appropriate corrective action to resolve the overallocation, which should result in cancelling or postponing projects, then it is important this information is added to your platform and you set up a regular monthly review and update of your heatmap process.

If you wish to start, change or stop a set of activities, you can see the impact on resources and plan reallocation where necessary, which provides the flexibility that many organisations want or need.

RESOURCE PLANNING IS CRITICAL

Proper planning prevents poor performance — or so the saying goes. Detailed planning is required to ensure any strategic initiative can be properly executed. Planning is the professional skill possessed by the project manager. It is their stock in trade. Any seasoned and competent project manager should be able to lead your strategic initiative, and in doing so they should be more than capable of working out how the initiative will be implemented, what people and skills are needed at what time and also identify the potential risks that may bring the implementation unstuck.

Most project managers develop their plan based on two critical theories: the theory of constraints[32] (ToC), which is summed up well within Eliyahu Goldratt's book *The Goal*[33], and the second, a technique called critical path method[34]. These theories allow the creation of a plan based on looking at the whole system as one, and assessing the necessary tasks or process and the logical sequence required to deliver the strategic initiative. These theories help the project manager and implementation team assess and determine all that is needed to achieve the required outcomes of the strategy being implemented and in doing so deliver the desired benefits in an environment of scarce resources. Initiatives succeed or fail based upon the availability of the right skills at the right time, and where these people are not available, the initiative slows down or stops entirely.

Given the complexities involved in this planning process, we recommend you use a technology platform. Microsoft Excel will not allow the dynamic cross-team allocation analytics you need to make informed resourcing decisions. There are many excellent technology platforms you can use to support this activity. Most of our clients already use Microsoft Project so we tend to leverage the information they already have, as well as the licences, and use Microsoft Project Online[35].

Regardless of the platform you use, our belief is one of the keys to success is having all your team members within the platform and assigned to an aggregated delivery schedule. It allows you to view who is working on all programs, projects and tasks.

TEMPORARY WORK REQUIRES TEMPORARY RESOURCES

One of the unique challenges that comes with project-based work is the human resources function. Unlike operational or BAU work, project-based resources come and go from project to project. Contractors and other temporary or non-ongoing workers often provide the personnel requirement for any project or strategic initiative. They are brought on for a specific project for a set period of time, and then let go once the project is delivered. Organisations run aground when they try to manage a variable workload of projects and initiatives that are starting and ending at various times, with a fixed workforce that doesn't really change.

While the use of contractors or temporary staff may come at a higher cost when compared to salary-based, ongoing staff, project-based workers develop specific skills and experiences delivering specific initiatives and take that set of skills from organisation to organisation somewhat like itinerant workers. The benefit of contractors however, is that you can scale up and scale down as needed, and the individuals involved can be brought into your organisation for a specific period and then at the end, they leave. This means you don't have to increase your overall headcount or take on a higher salary liability.

Do you have visibility of what your resources are doing?

---

[32] https://en.wikipedia.org/wiki/Theory_of_constraints
[33] https://en.wikipedia.org/wiki/The_Goal_(novel)
[34] https://en.wikipedia.org/wiki/Critical_path_method
[35] https://products.office.com/en-au/project/project-online-premium

Chapter XVIII

KEEPING TRACK AND KEEPING SCORE

Targets are one of the most critical items to address when it comes to achieving your strategic objectives, but also one of the hardest things to get right. You only have to look at the various regulatory issues that financial corporations are facing — continuous "errors" for which customers and the regulator are receiving compensation — and the associated negative press.

Balance Scorecard (BSC), looks at four key areas of your business: financial, customer, internal business processes, and organisational capacity. The benefit in using this model is the added focus on the three non-financial areas. This will help you reduce the over-emphasis on financial metrics so common across all industries, and assist with the project delivery environment as well.

I hear you asking, how are the correct targets set, or can I improve the targets I set for my team or organisation? From our experience and research, we have found that most companies set very narrow targets that drive the short-term behaviour, as with the example of the financial institutions who set only financial targets and which resulted in significant customer issues. If they had set customer targets and ensured they were taken seriously over the long term, this would have significantly reduced customer complaints.

We recommend targets are set at three levels: individual, team, and organisational; and that they are weighted towards long-term outcome-based results as well as shorter-term output-based results. For example, your sales team may have a new customer target — there should also be a satisfaction target for these new customers as they come into your company and are serviced by other teams. A team-based target comes in with the other teams' service. Team-based targets could be in support of each other, cross-business leads, or similar. At the organisation level an actual growth target should be your focus rather than new customers, because if you are losing more customers than gaining, then you will not last long as an organisation or in your job.

It is obviously important to also measure your organisation's performance against these targets as you work through each financial year. We recommend you review achievement of targets on a quarterly basis and update where necessary. Updating targets has to be done carefully, especially where commissions and bonuses are in play.

At the individual level, targets must be aligned to your team's roles. This is where, in our experience, organisations often go wrong, partly due to teams undertaking more or different responsibilities than they have in their position or role descriptions, and partly due to the targets not being aligned to these roles. For example, they are supporting a program or project, but their measures are all focused on their group, division, or business-area success.

All these targets should not be purely focused on financial return. In fact, a financial return may be not applicable as you are focused on health and well-being or environmental such as reducing climate change. With these non-financial goals, it is still critical to have measures in place to prove they have been achieved. With health this could be based on a reduction in cause of flu, cancer or type-2 diabetes in the next 10 years. Environmental goals could include achieving a net carbon zero level by mid-century.

Recognition of the part you played in achieving these targets is a bonus and leveraging this and your success will assist you to work on additional and new goals.

On top of metrics and transparency of progress, one other key item is the alignment of compensation and the need to ensure you have set lead-based measures, not just lag.

The lead indicators must focus on the intent or goal. They should be outcome-focused and future-looking and allow gate assessments to look forward and ask the question, is this initiative still worthwhile? This is opposed to a backwards-facing approach of "we have invested significantly already so we have to keep going".

Chapter XIX

GOLDEN RULES OF LEADERSHIP

Leaders such as yourself need to inspire your team, motivate them into action and walk the talk when it comes to culture. You need to maintain a strong influence over programs, projects and BAU activities. Therefore, a collaborative approach to leadership, where co-design is used to create a common purpose, is critical to success. This is not the same as managing your team, and unfortunately, we often see organisational leaders managing. They focus down into their organisation on tasks and firefight, rather than purpose-setting and gaining commitment.

The table below published by John Kotter's *A force for Change: How Leadership differs from Management* will help you work out if you or your leaders are leading and managers managing.

MANAGEMENT **Produces Order & Consistency**	**LEADERSHIP** **Produces Change & Movement**
Planning and Budgeting • Establish agendas • Set timetables • Allocate resources	**Establish Direction** • Create a vision • Clarify big picture • Set strategies
Organising and Staffing • Provide structure • Make job placements • Establish rules and procedures	**Aligning People** • Communicate goals • Seek commitment • Build teams and coalitions
Controlling and Problem-solving • Develop incentives • Generate creative solutions • Take corrective action	**Motivating and Inspiring** • Inspire and energise • Empower subordinates • Satisfy unmet needs

This inward focus causes issues with the managers, as they are displaced from their roles, so they tend to adopt a micro-management style to add value, and this obviously causes issues with those trying to get tasks done. They feel they are continually reporting to the manager rather than getting the job done.

Leadership is about sense-making and selecting an appropriate approach to different situations. Therefore, role clarity for your leaders is critical, as is measuring the effectiveness of your role and theirs. You should be measured on their ability to lead, or manage, depending on your level in your organisation, using a clearly defined leadership skills model.

The leadership skills must allow executives to make informed decisions about your organisation's goals and outcomes, and be able to properly allocate resources to achieve those outcomes. Delegation is therefore a critical skill along with being trustworthy, accepting feedback both positive and negative, and taking responsibility for successes and failures.

Setting your organisational direction should not be done by just an individual executive. You must have a vision and mission, but be able to include your team in owning parts or all of it so it is shared and uniting at your level. Too often we come into organisations to help and find it is the executives who are the challenge as they are not aligned to a common purpose and set of goals and outcomes.

Where this is the case, we recommend you support the executives in bringing their needs to the table and help them understand that as a team there is also the collective needs of your organisation, which will sometimes compete with their individual needs, so they may lose out on an optimal approach to allow your organisation as a whole to achieve more or a greater outcome.

We use a technique of longtable and roundtable to assist with these discussions. The long table represents your divisional executives' requirements, only looking at what is best for their group or division, that is, not taking into account the needs of other groups or divisions. As mentioned before this is unfortunately where it often stops.

Moving the culture and thinking of your executives to hearing needs of other executives, via a round table, or system-of-system view, should help them better understand what trade-offs are needed for your organisation as a whole to succeed.

It is important here that your executives' performance metrics are also updated to reflect any cross-group, division or business unit support that has been agreed, so their performance is measured on what is best for your organisation and not just their individual silos.

Clarity of tasks aligned to outputs, which are used to create outcomes, over time create the benefits you and your organisation are seeking. It will be easier to adjust the metrics and therefore associated behaviours of your executives, who in turn will have their teams working on aligned tasks that will help the executives, and you, succeed as top performers.

Drucker, the great management thinker, wrote "... you can't manage what you can't measure". Having the right measurements in place lets you know whether or not success has been achieved collectively and individually.

To better align to the collective goals, having transparency of these metrics significantly assists with executives working together. With the right culture they are able to help each other achieve their individual goals. This should be a metric that is being measured as well.

How visible are your performance metrics to your team?

If they are not visible we recommend sharing them with your team, as they will be able to better support you achieve them as well as better understand some of the decision you make driven by these metrics.

Chapter XX

WHAT'S THE DIFFERENCE IN YOUR APPROACH?

All too often we are asked by clients to review their programs and projects so we can help them improve their success rate, which unfortunately has been at 60% to 70%. All projects within large companies over the past 20 years have been challenged[36]. As you know there has been significant investment in project management frameworks and establishment of PMOs and TMOs (transformational management offices), but this has yet to improve this statistic.

One reason we believe this to be the case is that these methods are now measuring more, so we are more likely to know and record if a project has been successful or not. The other driver is the external environment into which projects deliver. This has become more volatile, uncertain, complex and ambiguous, resulting in projects needing to adapt and change to meet emerging requirements. As these requirements were not known at the start of the project, they often cause the project to run over cost or budget and often both.

To ensure it is different this time, we recommend following a proven principle-based approach covering your organisation's purpose, people, practices, platforms and performance. Each of these elements ensures you are considering your organisation as a whole and checking in to confirm strategic objectives are achieved in the most efficient and effective way.

To assess what needs to change to be fully aligned with these principles, we have developed an assessment based on an enhanced IPMA ICB4®, PROSCI® PCT, P3M3® model[37]. This assessment also includes the critical people, and external or emergent elements. By understanding your maturity today and defining your industry or best possible target maturity of the future and the benefits in having this maturity, you are able to ensure you not only deliver your current set of projects but also improve the environment into which these projects deliver, thus improving their chances of success.

From our experience there are some key improvements you can make that will drive your overall organisational strategy implementation maturity to a higher level. They involve putting in place the right governance and controls.

On the governance side, we recommend ensuring you have sufficient representation on your steering committees of business executives who will operate the outputs of projects. This is where program management comes to the forefront. By having them involved in the decision-making process you are able to gain their regular commitment and input to optimising what is delivered to maximise the value to your organisation.

The controls we would recommend are defined decision points such as stage gates. We would recommend no initiative, however large, runs for more than three months without a formal go/no-go decision made by its sponsor or business owner with the input from these business executives. That way, projects unlikely to deliver the intended value initially expected can be stopped or changed, rather than continuing until they run out of funding or the project manager leaves.

At these gates it is critical that your sponsor has their organisational performance metrics aligned to achieving the goals or objectives of the initiative/s they are sponsoring. To do this they will also need a valid and approved business case and plan.

It is also important someone independent to the initiative supports these gate assessments. Preferably someone who is able to objectively review progress and independently report their confidence in the initiative. We would recommend your PMO performs this role.

Your PMO can check the validity of the plan and business case, including the approach to estimating. Poor estimates are a common driver to project failure. The SIO is also able to aggregate all your relevant initiatives' metrics into a dashboard, which it can talk to at your executive meetings.

This forward view will also need to assess the level of risk your organisation is taking on to achieve the goal, and how these are to be managed. Risks are typically ill managed, with most organisations taking on too many initiatives and so lacking time to undertake effective risk management. By having accurate estimates and a clear intent, risks to achieving one or both can be assessed more accurately, and appropriate treatment put in place.

All of these activities take time and effort and require your team to have the right level of competencies once you have created a goals-oriented culture, which should be thought of as a set of habits or rituals carried out by your teams and championed by your sponsors.

For your sponsors to champion their initiatives, and be able to support their success, active sponsorship is critical, and we therefore recommend each person does not sponsor more than three initiatives. The mix of initiatives should also not include all of the most challenging and complex initiatives, but a blend at different phases within their delivery lifecycle.

Where you have delegation issues, that is, your sponsor has many projects but can't delegate due to a financial delegation limit, we recommend having an executive sponsor with this financial approval, and a prime sponsor actively involved in decision making on the program or project.

We have been engaged by many large organisations to "rescue" programs and although we always turn them around, when reviewing the program against its original business case, we have not been involved with a rescued program that has delivered to its original business case time or budget. Our view in situations like these is that although the program or project may deliver its objectives, calling it successful is probably a stretch and it is best to set these programs up for success and reset regularly so they do not veer off path and need rescuing.

Now is the time for you as an authentic business leader to step forward and take charge in ways that business schools don't teach.

Vision — Today's business leaders need the ability to see through the chaos and have a clear vision for their organisations. They must define the "true north" of their organisation: its mission, values, and strategy. They should create clarity around this true north and refuse to let external events pull them off course or cause them to neglect or abandon their mission. It must be their guiding light. Unilever CEO Paul Polman, who we referenced earlier, has done this especially well by focusing the company's true north on sustainability.

Understanding — With your vision in hand, as a leader you need in-depth understanding of your organisation's capabilities and strategies to take advantage of rapidly changing circumstances, playing to your strengths while minimising your weaknesses. Listening only to information sources and opinions that reinforce your own views carries great risk of missing alternative points of view. Instead, you need to tap into myriad sources covering the full spectrum of viewpoints by engaging directly with your customers and employees to ensure you are attuned to changes in their markets. Spending time in the marketplace, retail stores, factories, innovation centres, and research labs, or just wandering around offices talking to people, is essential.

Courage — Now more than ever, you need the courage to step up to these challenges and make audacious decisions that embody risks and often go against the grain. You cannot afford to keep your head down, using traditional management techniques while avoiding criticism and risk-taking. In fact, your greatest risk lies in not having the courage to make bold moves. This era belongs to the bold, not the meek and timid.

Adaptability/Agility — If ever there were a need for leaders to be flexible in adapting to this rapidly changing environment, this is it. Long-range plans are often obsolete by the time they are approved. Instead, flexible tactics are required for rapid adaptation to changing external circumstances, without altering strategic course. This is not a time for continuing the financial engineering so prevalent in the past decade. Rather, you need multiple contingency plans while preserving strong balance sheets to cope with unforeseen events.

Agility is critical because strategic adjustments must be made continually.

---

[36] http://www.standishgroup.com/outline
[37] https://en.wikipedia.org/wiki/P3M3

Chapter XXI

BUILDING YOUR IMPLEMENTATION PLATFORM

Whether you like it or not, as a high-performing executive, technology is a core part of your role. In this digital era, technology is playing a major part in almost everything we do. Your team currently performing routine work are unlikely to have a role in the future, with computers able to do their jobs faster, cheaper and more effectively. We are also seeing design take on a greater role than ever in the past, with global consultancy companies acquiring design houses. They see their value and market shrinking due to the ability of organisations to engage directly with their customers and therefore not require third parties to help them define their customer needs.

You are in the technology game

Technology has allowed the mobilisation of a global workforce to which routine or non-complex tasks can be outsourced to a developing country with much lower labour rates, resulting in savings of up to 70%. As a result, we are seeing our primary economic drivers change from owning land to owning factories to now creating, owning and licensing intellectual property (IP). The value of many of the largest global companies is no longer based on tangible assets, but instead is based upon their IP. If you look at today's most successful companies such as Facebook, Uber and Airbnb, they have a high level of investment and innovation in technology. They invest in the creation of IP rather than in creation or maintenance of physical assets. Facebook creates no content, Uber does not own cars and Airbnb does not have any property — instead they create a platform that allows buyers and sellers to interact.

Reliable, high-speed internet connections have created a new opportunity. We are seeing many organisations move from on-premises software (on-prem)[38], where they buy their infrastructure and applications and manage themselves, to cloud-computing services[39] in the form of software as a service (SaaS), platform as a service (PaaS) and infrastructure as a service (IaaS). This has allowed better quality software and hardware services at a lower cost. These services are core to the providers' business and they can pass on multi-use infrastructure scale-based savings as well as allow the organisation to purchase software on a monthly basis.

In the modern organisation, we have platforms and systems for an array of functions. We operate financial systems, human resource systems and payroll systems. With most organisations spending as much as 30% of their revenue on implementation, it makes perfect sense to have a strategy implementation system as well.

Platforms are the future

You may have been shown software platforms that claim to do everything. There are one or two organisations that are incredible at selling the sizzle of what their platform can do and then position the cost of only a small part, so when you want to fully integrate it with your enterprise environment the costs mount significantly. From our experience, having a strategy implementation platform is critical and most providers fall well short of providing this holistic approach. We have found most current software providers have started with solving project management issues and grown up, so as a consequence their whole architecture is project-centric and not focused on your organisation as a whole.

I hear you asking, why do we think a software platform is critical? The main reason is it ensures your team actually keep their promises by transparently displaying their progress to achieving your organisational strategic objectives. Now think about this and your current software platform. Does it answer this critical question: how are you progressing to achieving your strategic objectives? I am sure you are thinking, we can, but we have to pull information from various sources and there is a lot of manual work to achieve this visibility. If this is the case, then your platform is not providing what you need to fully manage your business.

A platform allows you to improve consistency. Learning from experience optimises the approach to delivering your strategic objectives and improves the quality of the management of your organisation.

Creating management dashboards

At steering committee or board meetings we often see members grappling with currency of information issues. By the time a report filters its way through the management levels up to the board, it is often a few weeks if not months old, and as such, decisions are often too late or already made. You are also faced with stopping things that should not have started in the first place. So please make sure you include currency of information, and determine when it needs to be up to date, the end of the day, week, month, quarter, year or always?

It is important for you to think through what information you need to operate effectively and to assess what other high-performing organisations do. Perhaps even your supplier may have more mature platforms then you and you can learn what you need from its approach. Having this view of the ideal will help you continuously improve, but remember as you improve so do others and the applications/platforms, so you will need to regularly review to keep your target operating model or blueprint at optimal levels.

A word about data security

With the move to technology, one of the biggest issues we are seeing is executives facing more scrutiny. You would have read in the press of data breaches, which are becoming more frequent as illustrated by Information is Beautiful[40] so you need to be mindful of your providers and those handling your data. You will see many breaches are from backup or where access has been given to an unauthorised person.

Although breaches are becoming more frequent, these companies'
existence depends on ensuring your data is safe, and they employ large
numbers of security experts to help. So, our view is you are still better
off in the cloud and storing your data with professionals then having
on-prem storage and a small team responsible for security, which we
often find is only one of their many duties.

---

[38] https://en.wikipedia.org/wiki/On-premises_software
[39] https://en.wikipedia.org/wiki/Cloud_computing
[40] http://www.informationisbeautiful.net/visualizations/worlds-biggest-data-breaches-hacks/

Chapter XXII

IMPLEMENTATION –
MAKING IT ALL HAPPEN

Thank you for getting to this point, we hope you have found the content of this book useful and it helps you, your team and your organisation increase performance in a measurable way.

We have covered a lot of content, so it would be remiss of us to stop here without providing you with an approach to implement what we have discussed throughout this book. Here is our process to help you get on your way.

Leveraging what you have read in this book, we propose you tailor your approach to transforming your organisation beginning with understanding why: why the program is being done and where you can add most value as well as DELIVER immediate results through our proven approach, outlined below.

- **D**iscover and diagnose the issues and opportunities using proven techniques including establishing a working group, interviews, and review of existing materials.
- **E**xamine the opportunities and gaps by linking issues/ opportunities to the changes/solutions needed to achieve the benefits, and prioritise these on the value, risk/reward to your appetite for change.
- **L**earn from what has worked before by listening to your peers, staff and customers as well as attending conferences and professional association events. By understanding where historical challenges have been and using lessons learnt from past events you should be able to tailor the solution to the needs of your organisation. We have learnt from experience and research that improved maturity is directly linked to fewer defects and issues, lower costs and faster delivery.
- **I**mplement the programs using a holistic, adaptive and iterative approach, focusing on outcomes and benefits.

- **V**alidate the effectiveness of the program through feedback forms and discussions, answering the question, are we doing the right things?
- **E**valuate where changes and improvements can be made including the process efficiency (lean thinking), information/knowledge management and tech involvement, based on what you have delivered.
- **R**einforce and revisit the five principles gaining agreement on future program delivery format and timings until achieving a maturity level to meet your needs.

To ensure you are delivering maximum value, we recommend you define broader business objectives to which you align. Remember:

- **Purpose** — Ensure the vision is clear, understood and the teams being coached and trained are working towards it.
- **People** — Equip your staff for the changes needed to meet future work practices through focused development opportunities, advice and offerings.
- **Practices** — Develop key skills that will remain relevant and valuable, and enjoy personal growth, whatever the future brings. At the same time, reskill people so they can embrace new directions and have the best chance of success tomorrow.
- **Platform** — Digitise work to reduce cost, improve quality, provide transparency, reduce risk and maximise outcomes and benefits.
- **Performance** — Measure performance against the above purpose/vision/mission, using lead-based metrics, so you can be confident the tasks being undertaken are on track to deliver the required results.

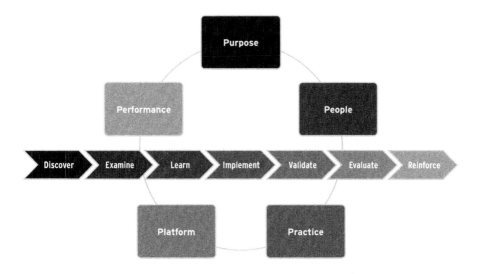

Establishing the new way of working and embedding many of the concepts and practices we have discussed throughout this book takes both leadership and discipline. To make it happen requires you to create the energy to start and sustain this transformation over two or three years. This is a journey that will yield great rewards, but will also test the mettle of the most seasoned executive.

We wish you the very best of success in your quest to implement your strategy.

Thank you for reading *The Strategy Implementation Gap*. I hope you gained some useful insights into delivering your strategic goals in a sustainable way.

While writing and publishing it, I received many requests for help in using a digital platform to improve collaboration.

Over the past three years, with the support of clients, we have developed even better offerings to improve business practices.

This development is especially acute with the COVID-19 virus totally changing the way we work and interact with each other.

To assist with those requests I have written another book, *Leading Your Digital Transformation With Microsoft's Collaboration Apps*.

It will help you and your teams leverage the Microsoft collaboration tools to support modern and rapidly evolving work practices.

As you may remember from *The Strategy Implementation Gap*, online collaboration involves managing benefits, risks, actions, decisions, dependencies, issues, changes, assumptions, lessons learnt all set up in PMLogic's fully configured Strategy Implementation Platform – in short, B-RADICAL. I hope you enjoy my new offering.

LEADING YOUR DIGITAL TRANSFORMATION WITH MICROSOFT'S COLLABORATION APPS

by James Bawtree

James Bawtree

James is passionate about contributing to the project management arena. Working with people shaping strategy and delivering meaningful results underpins his desire to foster quality excellence and world-class innovation. With 20 years' experience, James started his career at Rolls-Royce PLC, later to qualify as a Chartered Professional Mechanical Engineer (CPEng) and recently, as a well-known project leader, as a Chartered Project Professional (ChPP). James is a globally certified transformation practitioner (AgileSHIFT®) and change manager (PROSCI) as well as a globally approved PMO (P3O®), program (MSP®) and project management (PRINCE2 Agile®) trainer, coach and mentor. He is a National Board Member of the Australian Institute of Project Management, has led multiple MBA modules in strategy implementation, and enjoys delivering programs using the latest Microsoft collaborative technology.

Michael Young

Michael is a leading international expert in project management, and strategy and its implementation. Michael has worked with ISO, Standards Australia, the International Project Management Association and Australian Institute of Project Management. Some of Australia's leading organisations have engaged his services to "get clear on their strategy" and to ensure it is successfully executed. His work has been featured in BRW, the Australian Financial Review, the Sydney Morning Herald, The Age and the Canberra Times. Michael is passionate about creating a sustainable future. He has spoken on this topic around the world and was recently invited to the United Nations Global Business Leader Forum.

Printed in Great Britain
by Amazon

77884379R00120